Science Learning and Inquiry with Technology

When implemented effectively, technology has great potential to positively connect with learning, assessment, and motivation in the context of K–12 science education and inquiry. Written by leading experts on technology-enhanced science learning and educational research, this book situates the topic within the broader context of educational psychology research and theory and brings it to a wider audience. With chapters on the fundamentals of science learning and assessment, integration of technology into classrooms, and examples of specific technologies, this concise volume is designed for any course on science learning that includes technology use in the curriculum. It will be indispensable for student researchers and both pre- and in-service teachers alike.

Diane Jass Ketelhut is Associate Professor of Teaching and Learning, Policy and Leadership at the University of Maryland, USA.

Michael Shane Tutwiler is Assistant Professor of Educational Foundations at the University of Rhode Island, USA.

Ed Psych Insights

Series Editor: Patricia A. Alexander

Assessment of Student Achievement
Gavin T. L. Brown

Self-Efficacy and Future Goals in Education
Barbara Greene

Self-Regulation in Education
Jeffrey A. Greene

Strategic Processing in Education
Daniel L. Dinsmore

Cognition in Education
Matthew T. McCrudden and Danielle S. McNamara

Emotions at School
Reinhard Pekrun, Krista R. Muis, Anne C. Frenzel, and Thomas Goetz

Teacher Expectations in Education
Christine M. Rubie-Davies

Classroom Discussions in Education
Edited by P. Karen Murphy

Science Learning and Inquiry with Technology
Diane Jass Ketelhut and Michael Shane Tutwiler

DIANE JASS KETELHUT AND
MICHAEL SHANE TUTWILER

Science Learning and Inquiry with Technology

NEW YORK AND LONDON

First published 2018
by Routledge
711 Third Avenue, New York, NY 10017

and by Routledge
2 Park Square, Milton Park, Abingdon, Oxon, OX14 4RN

Routledge is an imprint of the Taylor & Francis Group, an informa business

© 2018 Taylor & Francis

The right of Diane Jass Ketelhut and Michael Shane Tutwiler to be identified as authors of this work has been asserted by them in accordance with sections 77 and 78 of the Copyright, Designs and Patents Act 1988.

All rights reserved. No part of this book may be reprinted or reproduced or utilised in any form or by any electronic, mechanical, or other means, now known or hereafter invented, including photocopying and recording, or in any information storage or retrieval system, without permission in writing from the publishers.

Trademark notice: Product or corporate names may be trademarks or registered trademarks, and are used only for identification and explanation without intent to infringe.

Library of Congress Cataloging-in-Publication Data
Names: Ketelhut, Diane Jass. | Tutwiler, Michael Shane, author.
Title: Science learning and inquiry with technology / Diane Jass Ketelhut, Michael Shane Tutwiler.
Description: New York, NY : Routledge, 2018. | Series: Ed psych insights | Includes bibliographical references and index.
Identifiers: LCCN 2017036639 (print) | LCCN 2017037785 (ebook) | ISBN 9781315522975 (e-book) | ISBN 9781138696938 (hardback) | ISBN 9781138696945 (pbk.)
Subjects: LCSH: Science—Study and teaching (Elementary) | Science—Study and teaching (Secondary) | Inquiry-based learning.
Classification: LCC LB1585 (ebook) | LCC LB1585 .K476 2018 (print) | DDC 372.35/044—dc23
LC record available at https://lccn.loc.gov/2017036639

ISBN: 978-1-138-69693-8 (hbk)
ISBN: 978-1-138-69694-5 (pbk)
ISBN: 978-1-315-52297-5 (ebk)

Typeset in Joanna MT
by Apex CoVantage, LLC

Dedication

In loving memory of Diane's father, Dr. Herman Earl Jass. He nurtured her lifelong passion for science and science education. Herman loved to engage in scientific discourse, which helped Diane refine and develop her own theories. He was eager to see this final product, but unfortunately passed away prior to its completion. His scientific curiosity remains with Diane forever.

Contents

List of Illustrations   viii

    Introduction   **1**
    Diane Jass Ketelhut

One: **Science Learning Issue #1: Learning Real Science**   **7**

Two: **Science Learning Issue #2: Assessment**   **33**

Three: **Science Learning Issue #3: Motivation**   **64**

Four: **Implementing Technologies Into Science Classrooms**   **84**

Glossary   113
Acknowledgments   117
Index   118

Illustrations

FIGURES

2.1. The Relationship between Learning, Teaching,
and Assessment — 36

2.2. Revised Bloom's Taxonomy — 43

2.3. Scientopolis — 59

2.4. Tool Use in SAVE Science — 59

4.1. The TPACK Theoretical Framework — 94

TABLES

1.1. Mapping River City Activities onto Scientific Inquiry
Processes — 28

4.1. Example of Stages in the SAMR Framework — 101

Introduction

Diane Jass Ketelhut

I was standing in a community forum line to register to vote on funding for a new school. The school had already been built, but now funding was needed primarily to supply it. From a practical perspective, it seemed to be a no-brainer to vote yes for funding, considering that we had already spent the money to build the school. I learned, standing in that line, that my perspective might have been clouded by my status as an educator. For while I stood there, the conversation around me was fairly uniform. I heard snippets about how the school system always had its hand out, how teachers were lazy because they wanted to teach to smaller numbers of students than was the norm in the speaker's childhood, and lastly, snippets questioning the need to buy supplies. This last comment was one that I have heard over and over again, particularly in regard to science supplies, since after all, there is a whole world out there that students could explore. As much as I wanted to rail against some of the comments, I realized that underlying them all is the belief that because "I went to school, I am qualified to critique education," and "I learned just fine, therefore, the way I was taught was perfect." This underlying tenet, peculiar to education that expertise is distributed by experience solely regardless of learning, does not seem to hold in the same way for other fields, and has often had devastating complications for education. I often imagine

2 Introduction

what a judge might say if the defendant overruled his judgment, using as a reason that he had been a defendant many times!

While one might debate whether this comparison is valid or whether experience equals expertise, there is no doubt that comparing how one was taught 30 years ago to today is fraught with difficulties. For example, growing up I believed that the *Jeopardy* champion must be the smartest person in the world, given all that he/she knew. Then, information was knowledge. The time it took to find an answer was prohibitive in many cases. Hence, unless you had a *Cheers*-like Cliff Clavin character sitting in the bar with you, loud debates over minutiae could go on forever with little hope for consensus, thus, raising *Jeopardy* champions, and yes, even Cliff Clavin, to a high status.

That's not true today. Information does not equal knowledge, as information is ubiquitous. Anyone with a smartphone can find an answer to almost any fact-based question in minutes. I watch *Jeopardy* now and wonder why we care that this person knows that piece of information when I could find the answer (or in the case of *Jeopardy*, the question) in almost the same amount of time it takes Alex Trebek to read it and the contestant to ring in and answer.

What we need to know today is how to evaluate that easily found information, how to problem solve, and how to collaborate. Teaching someone to memorize information is only going to put them on the road for a chance to win *Jeopardy*—and even then, those odds are pretty slim! Rather, what we want for our children is for them to be successful in a career, maybe even to be the next Bill Gates. But Bill Gates is a problem solver, a designer, and a creator of knowledge . . . not a memorizer of information. Thus, memorizing information will not get our children on the road to being Bill Gates.

Introduction 3

So, how do we move from that *Jeopardy* champion/20th-century mindset to a 21st-century one? That is a difficult path to walk, not only because of the temptation to replicate what we know like those voters I overheard years ago, but also because along that path are people hawking the next best solution to all of education's ills—which in today's world often tends to be a technology. In many cases, those hawkers are set on expounding the wonderful attributes of their product, but they are far less focused on how those attributes are going to solve specific problems. As a result, those hawkers offer potentially distracting detours toward our goal of 21st-century learning.

In this book, we walk the path toward a 21st-century mindset with the perspective of problem solving. Our context, indeed our passion, is science education. We explore what we think science education should look like and why, and the discrepancy between that and formal science education as it is practiced today. We delve into what is needed to resolve that difference, and the obstacles to those solutions. Finally, in each chapter, we will explore how various digital, immersive technologies might either provide a solution to our identified science education issue, or ameliorate an obstacle to a known non-technological solution.

We take a critical eye on the technologies, exploring how and why they might help, as well as what their limitations might be. We take the stance that technology should not be used just because it is there, but instead when and where they best fit into curricula to serve specific needs. For example, it would not make sense to replace an entire science unit on pollution with the video game SimCity simply because we can. However, careful use of the game throughout the unit can help to support and build upon key concepts, as well as

4 **Introduction**

engage and interest students who are traditionally demotivated by traditional science class activities. This alignment between technology and curriculum works best when care is chosen in selecting the supporting technologies. However at all times, our focus is on how to ameliorate issues in science education and improve science understanding and engagement.

To simplify the conversation, we are focusing on immersive, digital learning technologies, that is, those based in computers, smartphones, tablets, and so forth. Just as the goal of education has changed from information-gathering to critical thinking skills, the use of technologies in the classroom has also changed in recent years in similar ways. At the start of the use of digital technologies in schools, they were used primarily by the teacher for organization and presentation of information. This was the age of the *Jeopardy* champions, where information was king. Teachers could suddenly take attendance and grade efficiently. PowerPoint and projectors replaced blackboards to facilitate information transmission. Technologies became tools for efficiency in school. Meanwhile, their uses outside of school for fun or for informal learning kept evolving to become far more complex that the uses in school. In 2006,[1] the Federation of American Scientists concluded that computer and video games "can teach higher-order thinking skills such as strategic thinking, interpretative analysis, problem solving, plan formulation and execution, and adaptation to rapid change."

Those high-order thinking skills are the exact ones that we now need to prioritize in school. Thus, this would seem to make these immersive, digital technologies a great tool for classroom learning. Unfortunately, technology use for learning in school stagnated for much of the late 1900s, despite

Introduction 5

pressures from various stakeholders who, aware of the changing goals for education, pushed for changes in how technologies were used in school. I believe we are now seeing schools recognize that as learning needs move from accumulating information to the more complex skills of problem solving, evaluating, and collaborating, the affordances of technologies provide platforms for learning those, and also to give insights into how those are learned.

The vast majority of technology-in-education books present the technologies first, then talk about why they should be used. While there is a role for those approaches, they do not help teachers know when or why to use these technologies or technology designers/researchers in making design decisions for education-focused design/research work. This book reverses that trend by focusing first on current issues in science education, thinking through theory-based solutions to those issues, and discussing why those solutions are problematic. We then explore how immersive, digital technologies can facilitate those solutions to science education issues or ameliorate the obstacles.

We focus on three major categories of issues in science education: learning, assessment, and motivation. While these are obviously interrelated, we pull them apart initially to ease our discussion of them with a chapter devoted to each. We delve a bit into describing those issues, their possible solutions suggested by theory, and practical roadblocks to those solutions. Then, for each issue, we present evidence of various technologies with affordances to improve those issues or facilitate the solutions. We caution that example technologies are just that: examples. In some cases, we choose examples from well-researched technologies that offer good evidence for our claims, even though the specific example is no longer

6 Introduction

available. We want the reader to understand what aspects of a particular technology facilitated learning or motivation, not that a specific example technology worked. That is the generalizable learning from this book.

REFERENCE

1. Federation of American Scientists. (2006). *Harnessing the power of video games for learning.* Washington, DC.

One

Science Learning Issue #1

Learning Real Science

It makes sense to start our conversation on science education with the cognitive issues that are at the heart of most people's worry: understanding of science. We are continually bombarded with a list of statistics that are meant to alarm us, and indeed many of them *should* alarm us. For example, according to a survey by the National Science Board in 2014,[1] 24% of us think that the sun goes around the earth, a pre-Copernican idea, although even some ancient Greeks knew otherwise! Fifty-eight percent of those surveyed did not know about the big bang, and crucially for our health, 45% think that antibiotics can kill a virus. At a time when superbugs are evolving with no susceptibility to antibiotics, this last fact is particularly alarming, because most scientists agree that inappropriate use of antibiotics promotes the rise of superbugs. Using antibiotics to try and kill, futilely, a virus is the very definition of inappropriate use.

Clearly, we need a more scientifically literate populace. The question becomes, what are we doing wrong and how do we fix this? Of all the subjects that we teach in school, science should be the one that lends itself to an easy response to students' consistent questions of "why do I need to know this?" and "will I ever use this in real life?" That is *assuming* we teach it in a way to make these connections obvious. We submit that the difference between real science and textbook-based

8 Science Learning Issue #1: Real Science

school science is at the heart of the problem of a poorly scientifically educated populace. We unpack this contention in this chapter.

WHAT IS REAL SCIENCE?

Before we can talk about learning real science versus textbook science, it is crucial that we try and define 'real science.' For us, real science refers to science that is authentic to the field. Authentic work is sometimes described as: work that is "coherent, meaningful, and purposeful to the practitioners of the culture,"[2] or "The ordinary practices of the culture."[3] What does this mean for science? What are the ordinary practices of scientists?

It is intriguing that if you do an internet search for "practices of scientists," the top returns are all educational documents seeking to define scientific practices. It seems that scientists know what they are doing, but educators are in search of a way to operationalize it. So, in order to try and answer this question from the perspective of scientists themselves, it is more illuminating to search for images of scientists. Try it! Viewing hundreds of images of scientists, you see men, women, children, diverse races and ethnicities, and old black-and-white as well as modern colored photographs. The scientists are found in laboratories, out-of-doors, and even in coffee shops. Most telling is that in nearly every picture the scientists are observing, experimenting, analyzing, or collaborating. They are *actively* engaged in their work—work that is defined by Wikipedia as "a systematic activity to acquire knowledge that describes and predicts the natural world"—or what we are calling 'real science.'

Interestingly, we are all engaged in authentic scientific work every day. Whether one is trying to get the perfect foam top

Science Learning Issue #1: Real Science 9

for a cappuccino or growing a great crop of tomatoes without sharing with various garden pests, the activities of observing, experimenting, analyzing, and collaborating are always at work. Children in particular are always trying to understand their world. One only has to watch a baby drop a rattle off the side of a high chair over and over again to see them experimenting with object permanence and gravity. Every summer, children learn aspects of gravity, friction, force, and motion while trying to get the perfect run down a Slip 'n Slide. They may not be learning the actual terms, but on entering school, they will be familiar with their impact and effects. Once a learner understands the concepts and resultant cause and effects, terminology follows relatively easily. This learning of the concepts and how it works in the world is what we are identifying as real science. To summarize, then, being a real science participant means engaging in the practices of scientists and holding a strong conceptual understanding of how the world works.

REAL SCIENCE MEETS SCHOOL SCIENCE

So, if those images and descriptions are the practices of scientists, and if we do these practices in our daily lives, then we are constantly engaged in the practices of 'real science.' But, how does that differ from what happens in the K–12 classroom? Unfortunately, the amount of engagement in scientific practices that happens in K–12 varies greatly across the US. Even more troubling is that it varies by the racial and economic status of classrooms, which we will discuss more in a bit.

Bruce Alberts, a prominent biochemist and National Medal of Science awardee, has taken a strong interest in K–12 science education, particularly on the topic of real science. While

10   Science Learning Issue #1: Real Science

the editor in chief of *Science* magazine, he focused a number of his editorials on the state of K–12 science education. In one from 2012,[4] he remarked on what he saw as the shortcomings of 'school science':

> Those of us who are passionate about science have thus far failed to get real science taught . . . that difficult concepts are taught too early in the science curriculum, and they are taught with an overly strict attention to rules, procedure, and rote memorization . . . when we teach children about aspects of science that the vast majority of them cannot yet grasp, then we have wasted valuable educational resources and produced nothing of lasting value. Perhaps less obvious, but to me at least as important, is the fact that we take all the enjoyment out of science when we do so . . . Tragically, we have managed to simultaneously trivialize and complicate science education. As a result, for far too many, science seems a game of recalling boring, incomprehensible facts.

Clearly, he saw a big difference between science as he and his colleagues practiced it and the learning happening in K–12 science classrooms.

However, even assuming that we accept that there is a large separation between the two, is that wrong? Should *students* be engaged in real science, or is real science the province of scientists and informal explorers? At the heart of this question is really the purpose of school science: is the goal a knowledgeable citizenry or a larger pipeline for developing scientists? Throughout history these purposes have taken turns being centered, such as the focus on developing scientists during the post-Sputnik era.[5,6] However, how the purpose impacted

Science Learning Issue #1: Real Science   11

what was done in the classroom varied. As an example, the post-Sputnik era curricula focused on encouraging students to learn how to think like a scientist. This was instantiated by curricula that focused on both of the aspects of real science we have identified: engagement in practices and a strong conceptual understanding. Unfortunately, the goal of creating more scientists so overruled these curricula that included material was much too difficult.[7] In essence, these curricula left out one aspect: connecting to where the learner is. Bruce Alberts is clear in his editorial that simply requiring students to learn more complex materials without focusing on what they are ready to learn gains us nothing. We agree, and strongly take the position that these goals are tightly connected, and that in order to develop a citizenry with a strong conceptual understanding AND to produce large numbers of scientists, school science must integrate engagement in practices with developing conceptual understanding. But, it is crucial that school science recognizes the informal science explorer in each of us to avoid the errors of the post-Sputnik era.

Physicist Eric Mazur of Harvard University[8] states that students' intuitive understanding of physics based on their interactions in the real world is often in opposition to the physicist's understanding of the model- and formula-based world. This disconnect inhibits students' ability to connect their real-world explorations to formal scientific knowledge, and prevents them from understanding that they do science all the time. Think back to your own science classroom experiences; how many times did your teacher tell you to envision a world without friction before telling you a physics formula to explain a phenomenon in that world? Because none of us lives in such a world, we prevent children from taking their initial, possibly naïve/possibly accurate understanding of how the

12 Science Learning Issue #1: Real Science

world works and then growing those ideas into rich, scientifically sound conceptions. Instead, we frame science in such an abstruse way that non-scientists see it as something foreign, disconnected from their lives. It then becomes—as Alberts frames it—a "rote learning exercise."

THE ROLE OF SCIENTIFIC INQUIRY

So, how do we help children see the science in their own lives, and move from their naïve or pre-science conception of the world to one that is governed by a conceptual understanding of science? Studies indicate that exposure to scientific inquiry can help mediate this transformation.[9] And that leads us to the question: what is scientific inquiry? Go back to our Google search of the images of scientists. What we saw illustrated in those Google images—observing, experimenting, analyzing, collaborating—is scientific inquiry.

So, how does engaging in scientific inquiry help children develop a more scientifically accurate conception of the world, starting from their own explorations? Psychologists like the world-renowned Piaget suggest that we continually work to turn our experiences into some connected idea. You can think about this with the analogy of looking at an overwhelming pantry of food. In order to prevent complete confusion, each person observing this pantry will try and find a way to group what they see. Young children with little to no cooking experience to help chunk these items will make up some way to order things, possibly by color, shape, or container size. As we mature, we develop some new ideas that cause us to reframe our initial ordering. Thus, we might now see snacks, breakfast foods, and other 'stuff.' This continues all the way through to becoming a famous chef who might see particular sauce ingredients. Each new experience we have is

Science Learning Issue #1: Real Science 13

considered to see how it might fit into our original grouping. In general, we try to keep our original grouping, preferring to fit or even shoehorn our new experience into the ordering we already have instead of spending the mental energy to create new frameworks. Sometimes, we can't figure out how to do that, so we either reject the new experience or accept the need to change the original grouping. The goal of education is to help the learner know when to reject the new information, fit it into the existing construct, or use it to improve our mental models.

So, how does this relate to learning real science and scientific inquiry? In this analogy, the pantry supplies are bits of incoming information about how the world works. As young children investigating our world, we make up explanations for why things are the way they are. Sometimes those explanations are good beginning approaches, but other times, they are as useful as organizing our pantry into similar colors or shapes. Nonetheless, those initial groupings are *ours*, and thus ones we hold on to tightly. The secret is trying to figure out how to take the young child in the kitchen and turn him or her into a competent cook or even a chef. We can *tell* them how to do it without helping them develop the rationale for it, and in many cooking cases and certainly in schools, that is exactly what we do. This approach is the one that Alberts has railed against. Piagetian theory would suggest why Alberts is correct in denigrating this approach. Telling children what to do only causes them to try and shoehorn that new information into current mental models regardless of accuracy, or to reject the new information entirely.

If our goal is for learners to improve their mental models of how the world works based on their own initial, naïve conceptions, then we need to help them see for themselves that

14 Science Learning Issue #1: Real Science

sometimes there is a need to reorganize their thinking. *Telling* them they need to do this is one of the least effective ways to effect this change, as there is little motivation to overcome the initial resistance to change. Certainly all of us non-chefs can connect with that. Typically, we everyday cooks follow recipes (aka we are *told* what to do). As children, we might have played a bit with our food, particularly when our parents weren't watching, to develop some initial ideas of how things go together. Diane's grandson is famous for 'making soup,' which entails mixing together interesting things like applesauce, gummies, and cheese puffs into a bowl. While completely disgusting to us adults (!!), these are his initial attempts to learn about foods and how they mix and match. However, in learning to cook there is no connection between these initial learning experiences and the recipes we follow as adults; there is no way for him to take what seemed intriguing to him (for example, how different textures lead to interest in an entrée) and connect it to a recipe later on to allow him to improve on that recipe from what he already knows.

But, what if, instead, he continued to *play* in the kitchen, learning some basic foundational information while innovating with new ingredients? Hopefully, what he learned with his soup would enable him to progress to making soups that would be interesting to a broader audience than himself and his younger sister! He would then have a more solid mental framework on what to do with that pantry of supplies. Instead of only being able to cook a few recipes, he might be able to create an entire buffet from them!

This is the essence of how we need to learn science. When we *tell* children scientific information, it is no different than having them follow recipes. They cannot apply that information to new situations; they cannot connect it to the ideas they

Science Learning Issue #1: Real Science 15

already hold. It is no different than trying to turn that initial applesauce soup into something worthy of a dinner party. As Piaget said, without experimenting, we might get them to parrot back what we *tell* them akin to following a recipe verbatim, but they will not be developing conceptually strong scientific ideas founded on their own personal explorations. If instead we allow them to explore their own understanding in the science classroom, not unlike taking applesauce soup to the next level, learners might be able to develop more complex and scientifically sound conceptions. This exploration in the science classroom, as we discussed earlier, is scientific inquiry.

However, simply concluding that science education needs to be more fully organized around scientific inquiry is not enough. The call, indeed the clarion call, for scientific inquiry in the classroom is nearly as old as the field of science education. Various groups, scientists, and educators have seen a need to improve science education by continually suggesting for the last 150 years that scientific inquiry needs to play a larger role in science education.[5] Multiple policy reports over the past several hundred years have tried to identify what students need to understand about science, and in each, scientific inquiry has played a role. For example, Herbert Spencer wrote in 1860: "Children should be led to make their own investigations and to draw their own inferences."[10] The fact that we are still 'calling' for it as if it were a new idea indicates how difficult it is to recognize and apply in the classroom.

Over the last 20 years, each new report from the National Research Council, the Department of Education, and the American Association for the Advancement of Science has in some way continued to call for integration of scientific inquiry into the classroom, as if this were a new idea. For

16 Science Learning Issue #1: Real Science

example, the National Research Council has tried to make those connections in their report, *Taking Science to School*.[11] That report outlines four categories of knowledge that students need to understand to be "proficient in science." Aspects of scientific inquiry, as we have been defining it, can be seen in each of these categories, but most particularly in the second and fourth:

1. Know, use, and interpret scientific explanations of the natural world
2. Generate and evaluate scientific evidence and explanations
3. Understand the nature and development of scientific knowledge
4. Participate productively in scientific practices and discourse.[11]

The current national standards, the *Next Generation Science Standards*,[12] suggest that science instruction covers three main categories: science and engineering practices (encompassing what we are calling scientific inquiry), disciplinary core ideas, and crosscutting concepts, similar to the four categories of Taking Science to School.

So, if policy doctrines continue to push for scientific inquiry in the classroom as if it were a new idea, the implications are that we have been unsuccessful in following these recommendations. We argue here that this failure stems from three causes: lack of understanding of its potential, implementation of pseudo-inquiry, and uneven implementation across various school environments. We unpack these three issues next and then end this section discussing possible technological solutions.

Science Learning Issue #1: Real Science

Lack of Understanding of the Importance of Scientific Inquiry in the Classroom

Let's unpack why integrating scientific inquiry into the classroom is such a tough assignment and yet so necessary. The first issue is getting this into classroom practice consistently, which, unfortunately, still does not happen. Past research has indicated that 80% of K–8 schools do not teach science with hands-on interactive inquiry methods,[13] and there is little evidence that this has changed. This is particularly alarming, not just because it flies in the face of standards and recommendations, but this is also the age group where ideas about and interest in various topics are forming. Further, in these years, students are exposed to a very broad swath of science content. If we want to impact general science understanding in the public, it must happen during these years. By high school, students take only 1–3 years of science, and each year is focused on a particular slice of science content, where science content is broken up by discipline.

If our goal is to increase the public's conceptual understanding of science, then we are referring to more than their knowledge of discrete facts. Instead, we want them to understand big crosscutting ideas in science, such as evolution and energy. We want students to create strong mental models of these concepts on which they can connect specific ideas and facts. What happens in schools now is that while we organize science courses generally around these issues, the day-to-day lessons tend to focus more on the facts (e.g., the structure of the earth) that come together to describe the big ideas and less on the synthesis of those facts into the big ideas (e.g., geological change). So, as Bruce Alberts stated, children memorize those facts and regurgitate them on tests, but without

18 Science Learning Issue #1: Real Science

integrating those facts into ideas. Remember our discussion about Piaget. Students will not spend the energy to create new mental models without compelling motivation to do so. Thus, our ultimate goal of impacting their conceptual understanding is left behind.

So, imagine José entering school as a young child. While in daycare or at home, José has been playing and exploring his world. He watched his rattle fall off his high chair; he threw all sorts of objects (some to his teacher's dismay!) and observed their motion. All through these activities, José began to develop an understanding of motions of objects. Now, fast forward to José in school. By the end of the K–8 time period, José will have been asked to learn that a ball sitting still on the floor has lots of forces pushing on it, that a feather and bowling ball will hit the floor at the same time in a vacuum (and yes, he will be asked to learn the difference between his home use of 'vacuum' and the science use), and so forth. In some cases, these ideas and others will fit into what José has already started to understand about his world, but in others the discrepancies between what he knows and the teacher tells him will be too much for him to adjust to, and instead because he is a good student, he will memorize what the teacher tells him, but never change his thinking about how the world works. Really, did you expect him to just accept that a feather and bowling ball would hit the ground simultaneously in a world without air resistance? We often delude ourselves into thinking that good grades on tests indicate students' sound conceptual understanding.

Now, let's imagine a scenario where José studies science in a classroom where the teacher understands the major role that scientific inquiry could play. Rather than telling José how science conceives the world, this teacher creates an environment

Science Learning Issue #1: Real Science   19

where José plays with these ideas, tests out his own understanding to see if it still holds true, and then discusses his ideas with his classmates and teacher. If his own investigation causes him to question his understanding, then perhaps he might be willing to invest the energy needed to rethink what he had accepted as true, leading him toward more scientifically sound conceptions. If you are still unconvinced, put a bowl of water in a room, and ask some young children what they think it will look like tomorrow. Then, show them. If they believe that the water will still be there and then find it is not, ask them what they think happened to that water. Perhaps you will be amazed at their detailed reasons, possibly amused, but nonetheless you will start to understand how a young child thinks. In order to help them develop the understanding of evaporation, ask them to test out their inferences. Only when they have proved to themselves that a dog or giant has not drunk the water, or that the bowl does not have a hole in it, and so forth, will they open up to wanting to know more about this phenomenon.

This is an example of what is called a 'discrepant event,' in which students predict outcomes based on their own understanding, and then find their understanding sometimes called into question by experiments they themselves have designed and run. These powerful contradictions force students to rethink their understanding of the topic.[14] Having a teacher or other adult tell them the right answer does not have this same effect. What drives their change in thinking is the lack of coherence between what they thought should happen and what did happen. This encourages them to do that hard mental labor of reorganizing their conceptual frameworks.

This is why so many policy documents over the years have called for scientific inquiry to have a role in the classroom.

20   **Science Learning Issue #1: Real Science**

Unfortunately, the understanding of the role scientific inquiry plays in the classroom and the time and effort it takes to do it is often misrepresented. Some argue that the point of scientific inquiry in the classroom is just to have students mimic what scientists do to develop an authentic view of what being a scientist is. Others claim that there just isn't time in the schedule to conduct learning this way. But, really, can we afford not to spend some time making sure that students are truly developing more scientifically sound conceptions of the world? Clearly, those statistics of what the population understands of science indicates a failure in our current model. We need to help children make changes to their understanding, and scientific inquiry experiences (predicting, experimenting, analyzing) can drive this transformation. And really, how long would it take to put a bowl of water in the classroom and have a conversation on what will happen or did happen to it?

Misunderstanding of Scientific Inquiry in the Classroom

The second issue with consistent implementation of scientific inquiry in the classroom is a lack of common understanding of what constitutes classroom-based scientific inquiry. This issue was addressed in the design of the current Next Generation Science Standards, which decided not to use the term 'scientific inquiry' at all. In an early draft, the authors indicated that use of this term had become riddled with misunderstanding, resulting in curricular recommendations and teacher implementations that were often only scientific inquiry on the surface, not authentic instantiations of it. Thus, those standards designers chose to use scientific practices in lieu of scientific inquiry. Unfortunately, changing the term does not necessarily solve the issue of what scientific inquiry is, or how it should be implemented in the classroom. We

Science Learning Issue #1: Real Science   21

have chosen explicitly in this book to use the term 'scientific inquiry' because it allows us to connect the ideas in this book to the rich history of science and science education, which has consistently used that term. Previously in this chapter, we have described what scientific inquiry is, the work of scientists; thus in this section, we will discuss what it might look like in the classroom in contrast to what pseudo-scientific inquiry looks like.

Duvall[15] describes the inquiry-based science classroom as including both student-designed investigations into their own questions as well as learning content in service to understanding those investigations. The multiple policy descriptions of the recent past have mirrored this description. Unfortunately, how inquiry-based activities get translated in the classroom varies. If you visit a science classroom, you might see activities that march with Duvall's description, but equally likely, you might see recipe-type or what is sometimes called hands-on/ minds-off activities. Simply having students doing something besides listening and taking notes does not mean that students are engaged in scientific inquiry. The prior National Science Education Standards[16] offered a clear set of guidelines for engaging in scientific inquiry. These scientific activities include, but are not limited to, making observations, formulating hypotheses, gathering and analyzing data, and forming conclusions from that data. Many of these activities are mirrored in the science and engineering practices outlined in the current Next Generation Science Standards, as indicated earlier. Thus, following a step-by-step laboratory from a textbook falls far short of this description. While students might be making observations, they are rarely formulating hypotheses. They might be gathering data, but the analysis and conclusion drawing are far more often already explicitly stated in

22 **Science Learning Issue #1: Real Science**

the lab manual itself. As a result, the impetus for students to re-examine their mental frameworks is missing. These laboratories might serve a purpose of helping to explain a difficult concept, but they will not motivate a student to connect their own personal understanding of the concept with new information to forge a more scientifically accurate framework. Because the latter is the goal of education, these scientific inquiry 'light' explorations are insufficient in and of themselves to create greater science conceptual understanding.

Why, then, has 'scientific inquiry light' become more the norm than not in classrooms? The answer to that question is intricate. First, many teachers rely on textbooks as an authority, particularly those without a strong science background. Unfortunately, textbooks are a primary culprit in spreading pseudo-inquiry. The majority of them are vocabulary dense and activity-poor,[17] and included 'inquiry' activities often are low-level cognitive tasks.[18,19] Second, the reason many teachers rely on the textbooks is that they lack a strong science content understanding themselves. Research clearly indicates that the occurrence of scientific inquiry in the classroom is directly related to the science content expertise of the teacher.[18,20] Unfortunately, this problem is far more likely to occur in the lower grades that we indicated earlier was critically important for science education. K–8 teachers rarely have a major in a science field; depending on the state, the required science content courses for elementary certification can be minimal. Further, some states do not specify what science courses satisfy the elementary education requirement, so the content knowledge of an elementary teacher can vary widely. A third reason behind this problem of scientific inquiry light is that teachers tend to rely on their own teachers and their mentor teachers for models of how to teach.

Science Learning Issue #1: Real Science   23

This is only problematic in the case where the models tend to be very similar and contrary to recommendations. That is the unfortunate case in science education and helps maintain the culture of pseudo-inquiry. Finding a way to break this vicious cycle is key to changing the culture of science classrooms.

Equity of Access to Good Science Instruction

The third reason that scientific inquiry is not regularly found in all classrooms is an issue of equity. Students in low-level science classes or attending schools with high percentages of non-Asian minorities have far fewer opportunities to engage in scientific inquiry.[21] The reasons for this are complicated, and include limited resources and higher than normal percentages of inexperienced teachers for these schools/classes, and a prevalent view that these students need basic content first.[18,20,21,22] It is far more likely to find underresourced schools with high percentages of inexperienced teachers in urban environments with high percentages of non-Asian minorities than in suburban, primarily white school districts. Thus, we tend to see a 'scientific inquiry divide' between these sets of schools.

Some of the motivation behind the recent push for a national set of standards has been to try and offset the differences in opportunities between various school districts and student groups. It was felt that if all teachers and students were held to an agreed-upon list of what should be taught and learned, educational outcomes would improve. Unfortunately, for science understanding this has not been achieved in any consistently measurable way. The data is clear that the last 15–20 years of standards have not significantly improved science understanding from any number of different measures—either factual content or scientific process

24 Science Learning Issue #1: Real Science

understanding. We detail the issues in the much-discussed pipeline issue for science in Chapter 3, but it is a good example of the issue with equity of access to scientific inquiry. The inequities we see in scientific inquiry experiences for girls and non-Asian minorities reflects that seen as the pipeline narrows more so for these populations than others.[23] The standards themselves are not enough to initiate a transformation in the science classroom.

HOW CAN TECHNOLOGY HELP RESOLVE THIS ISSUE?

If, then, the path to increasing conceptual understanding is to find a way to get consistently more scientific inquiry into the classroom, then this is an arena with which technology can definitely help. While scientific inquiry has no intrinsic need to be conducted through computers, creating technology-based inquiry experiences can help mitigate some of the reasons for the lack of scientific inquiry discussed earlier. Over the past 20 years, quite a few designers and researchers have begun to create immersive experiences in computers and mobile technologies to provide a venue for students to conduct scientific inquiry. Depending on the design of these environments, they are referred to as games, serious games, virtual environments, and augmented reality.

So, what are immersive experiences? In an immersive experience, a participant feels as if they are participating in the activity. They develop empathy for the characters, a desire to solve problems, and a feeling as if it is real. As a middle schooler once said, comparing a 20-minute immersive experience to normal classroom problem-posing, "It seemed like a real life question—why is this happening? . . . not a made up question. . . [laughs] . . . Even though the game was made up, it felt like a real-life question." We started this chapter talking

Science Learning Issue #1: Real Science   25

about how science naturally lends itself to answering students' incessant questions of why they need to know something. As you can see from this quote, if designed well, students do not need to ask that question at all, as it is obvious why they need to know it. This student understood in this immersive experience that this was a problem she needed to solve to help fix the 'real world.' We will talk more about motivation to learn science in the next chapter, but even though this chapter is about conceptual understanding, it is impossible not to consider engagement, as no one will learn something if they do not spend time on task to do so. Therefore, motivation to learn is intrinsically bound to conceptual understanding.

OK, so how do immersive experiences like virtual worlds or computer games help with conceptual understanding? Primarily, these environments help mitigate the issues around getting scientific inquiry into the classroom, and we have discussed in detail in this chapter how scientific inquiry improves conceptual understanding. Remember that we indicated that three issues impeded consistent use of scientific inquiry in the classroom: lack of understanding of the importance of it despite policy recommendations, implementation of pseudo-inquiry in lieu of scientific inquiry, and uneven implementation across various school environments and school groups. In essence, what is needed from a possible solution, therefore, is something that allows students to conduct scientific inquiry-based investigations, provides a model for teachers on the value of and how to conduct scientific inquiry, and can be accomplished with diverse student populations in low-resourced schools. Quite a tall order! But, luckily, immersive environments seem to do much of this, according to research. Later we unpack this research on immersive environments, indicating the benefits, discussing

26 Science Learning Issue #1: Real Science

the obstacles, and then indicating where more research is needed.

Immersive environments are an ideal place to conduct scientific inquiry. Indeed, any computer game incorporates many of the attributes we have identified as scientific inquiry: exploration, investigation, data collection, and analysis. While off-the-shelf computer games use these skills for saving the princess, killing the dragon, conquering the castle, and so forth, in those designed for classroom use, those same skills can be linked for the purpose of problem solving and learning. To help explicate how immersive environments can embody scientific inquiry experiences for children, let's explore an example that both of us were part of the design team for: *River City* (http://muve.gse.harvard.edu/rivercityproject/). In *River City*, students take on the role of an epidemiologist, exploring why a 19th-century town has had a sudden increase in illnesses, and conducting experiments to identify the source(s) of the illnesses.[24]

In *River City*, students gather data from multiple sources, much like a real epidemiologist might do. They interview residents, talk to doctors about the frequency and types of illnesses, identify hot zones of illnesses, and sample water and flying insect populations—all to help understand the problem. They use initial data from these sources to create a hypothesis about the cause of illnesses in the town. Then, the technology allows them to create two River City environments, identical except for one change. They can thus do a controlled experiment, similar to many science fair projects, to evaluate their hypothesis. For example, if students have noted that there are many more mosquitoes near the bog and that the tenement homes built near the bog have a lot of fevers, they might hypothesize that the bog is promoting a mosquito-borne illness, identified

Science Learning Issue #1: Real Science   27

by fevers. In their controlled experiment, they might want to investigate what happens if the bog was filled in and dried up. In that case, one version of River City would have the bog as normal (what we might call the 'control treatment'), and the other version would be bog-free (the 'experimental treatment'). Students then collect the same data in each version, analyze that data, and draw conclusions about their hypothesis. Finally, they write a letter to the "Mayor of River City" outlining their investigation with recommendations for solving the problem. These are then shared in the classroom in a science conference format. To students' surprise, they discover that many of their classmates have identified different problems and have alternate recommendations. This allows the teacher to broker a discussion, helping students integrate their findings, and undermining the false idea that there is always one true answer to science experiments and problems.

So, is this scientific inquiry? Previously, we have indicated that both past and present national science standards state that scientific inquiry involves making observations, formulating hypotheses, gathering and analyzing data, forming conclusions from that data, and sharing and debating those conclusions. Table 1.1 shows how these map onto what students are doing in River City.

Clearly, based on this example of River City, these environments can address the issue of getting authentic, not pseudo, scientific inquiry into the classroom. However, for the other issues, the potential for these environments to effect change is less clear. Let's unpack what we learned in our work on River City. First, we have seen traditionally poorly performing students equal and indeed sometimes exceed their traditionally more successful and more content knowledgeable peers on selected measures of performance.[25] This outcome can help

28 **Science Learning Issue #1: Real Science**

Table 1.1 Mapping *River City* Activities onto Scientific Inquiry Processes

Scientific Inquiry Process	River City Behavior
Making observations	Exploring the environment Talking to residents
Formulating hypotheses	Using data gathered initially to create a hypothesis of the cause of illness
Gathering data	Water sampling Insect sampling Examining hospital records
Analyzing data	Taking data and averaging/graphing it
Forming conclusions from data	Writing report to mayor
Sharing/debating conclusions	Teacher facilitated classroom science conference

teachers understand that all students, identified as college-bound or not, can participate in scientific inquiry. Second, scientific inquiry is accessible via these environments, no matter what a school's resources are, because they only require a computer interface which is available throughout schools today.

The more problematic piece appears to be whether these immersive environments can provide models for teachers of what real scientific inquiry looks like, as described in Duvall.[14] While many of these environments were designed with this ultimate goal in mind, the data on whether they are successful for these purposes is minimal. On our work with *River City*, we have seen some teachers transform and others be

Science Learning Issue #1: Real Science   29

unaffected.[26] The game, *Quest Atlantis*, has modeling scientific inquiry for teachers as one of its explicit goals.[27] The evidence is not yet compelling on how successful this is.

Complicating this is that immersive environments/games tend to span the gamut of how scientific inquiry is operationalized, not unlike the broad array seen in textbooks. Some games offer interactivity that masquerades as inquiry. We have seen games (names are removed to protect the guilty!) advertise as an engaging interactive science environment, however, as players investigate the town, much of what they discover are textbook-like snippets to read. Their main activity is exploring the town, clicking on something, and reading. Given that science textbooks already confuse hands-on with 'minds-on' inquiry, adding a game that mimics this confusion hardly seems necessary. To contrast this to another internet-based game, Whyville (whyville.net) offers players several strong inquiry experiences built into a community forum.[28]

Based on this analysis, it would seem that there is a role for immersive environments in the classroom in providing models of good scientific inquiry, equity of access, and possibly models for improving teacher practice. However, as with anything, the solution is not simple, and even the best designed project is subject to how schools use them.

SUMMARY

In this chapter, we have presented the case that in order to improve both the conceptual understanding of the public and the number of students seeking to be scientists, school science must look more like real science. We argue that it is crucial that science education include scientific inquiry integrated into the learning process, and that this practice focus on helping students move from what they think they know

30 **Science Learning Issue #1: Real Science**

to a more scientifically sound conception. Even though policy doctrines support this approach, we will see in the next chapter that standards-based assessments among other issues are slowing the improvement. We offer that the use of immersive technologies like digital games can minimize some of the obstacles currently blocking a more widespread use of scientific inquiry.

REFERENCES

1. National Science Board. (2014). *Science and engineering indicators 2014.* Arlington, VA: National Science Foundation (NSB 14–01).
2. Griffin, M. M. (1995). You can't get there from here: Situated learning, transfer, and map skills. *Contemporary Educational Psychology, 20,* 65–87.
3. Brown, J. S., Collins, A., & Duguid, P. (1989). Situated cognition and the culture of learning. *Educational Researcher, 18*(1), 32–42.
4. Alberts, B. (1995). Panel urges shift of focus for school science courses. *Science Magazine.*
5. Deboer, G. E. (1991). *A history of ideas in science education: Implications for practice.* New York: Teachers College Press.
6. Duschl, R. (2008). Science education in three-part harmony: Balancing conceptual, epistemic, and social learning goals. *Review of Research in Education, 32*(1), 268–291.
7. Linn, M., Gerard, L., Matuk, C., & McElhaney, K. (2016). Science education: From separation to integration. *Review of Research in Education, 40,* 529–587.
8. Mazur, E. (2009). Farewell, lecture? *Science, 323,* 50–51.
9. Bybee, R. (2000). Teaching science as inquiry. In J. Minstrell & E. van Zee (Eds.), *Inquiring into inquiry learning and teaching in science* (pp. 20–46). Washington, DC: American Association for the Advancement of Science.
10. Spencer, H. (1860/1896). *Education: Intellectual, moral, and physical.* New York: D. Appleton and Co.
11. National Research Council. (2007). *Taking science to school: Learning and teaching science in grades K-8* (Committee on Science Learning, Kindergarten Through Eighth Grade, R. A. Duschl, H. A. Schweingruber, and A. W. Shouse, Eds.). Board on Science Education, Center for Education.

Science Learning Issue #1: Real Science 31

Division of Behavioral and Social Sciences and Education. Washington, DC: National Academies Press (*p. 2).

12. NGSS Lead States. (2013). *Next generation science standards: For states, by states.* Washington, DC: National Academies Press.

13. Jorgenson, O., & Vanosdall, R. (2002). The death of science: What we risk in our rush towards standardized testing and the three R's. *Phi Delta Kappan, 83,* 601–605.

14. Piaget, J. (1985). *The equilibration of cognitive structure.* Chicago: University of Chicago Press.

15. DuVall, R. (2001). Inquiry in science: From curiosity to understanding. *Primary Voices K-6, 10,* 3–9.

16. National Research Council. (1996). *National Science Education Standards.* Washington, DC: National Academy Press.

17. Leonard, W. H., & Chandler, P. M. (2003). Where is the inquiry in biology textbooks? *American Biology Teacher, 65*(7), 485–487.

18. Windschitl, M. (2004). Folk theories of "inquiry:" How preservice teachers reproduce the discourse and practices of an atheoretical scientific method. *Journal of Research in Science Teaching, 41*(5), 481–512.

19. Chinn, C., & Hmelo-Silver, C. (2002). Authentic inquiry: Introduction to the special section. *Science Education, 86,* 171–174.

20. Roehrig, G., & Luft, J. (2004). Constraints experienced by beginning secondary science teachers in implementing scientific inquiry lessons. *International Journal of Science Education, 26*(1), 3–24.

21. National Research Council (NRC) (2005). *America's lab report: Investigations in high school science.* Washington, DC: National Academies Press.

22. Marshall, J., & Dorward, J. (2000). Inquiry experiences as a lecture supplement for preservice elementary teachers and general education students. *American Journal of Physics, 68,* S27–S36.

23. Committee on Prospering in the Global Economy of the 21st Century: An Agenda for American Science and Technology, National Academy of Sciences, National Academy of Engineering, Institute of Medicine. (2007). *Rising above the gathering storm: Energizing and employing America for a brighter economic future.* Washington, DC: National Academies Press.

24. Ketelhut, D. J. (2007). The impact of student self-efficacy on scientific inquiry skills: An exploratory investigation in River City, a multi-user virtual environment. *Journal of Science Education and Technology, 16*(1), 99–111.

32 **Science Learning Issue #1: Real Science**

25. Ketelhut, D. J., Dede, C., Clarke, J., & Nelson, B. (2007). Studying situated learning in a multi-user virtual environment. In E. Baker, J. Dickieson, W. Wulfeck, & H. O'Neil (Eds.), *Assessment of problem solving using simulations* (pp. 37–58). Mahwah, NJ: Lawrence Erlbaum Associates.
26. Ketelhut, D. J., & Schifter, C. (2011). Game-based learning and teachers: Improving understanding of how to increase efficacy of adoption. *Computers and Education, 56,* 539–546.
27. Barab, S. A., Jackson, C., Piekarsky, E. (2006). Embedded professional development: Learning through enacting innovation. In C. Dede (Ed.), *Online professional development for teachers: Emerging models and methods* (pp. 155–174). Cambridge, MA: Harvard Education Press.
28. Galas, C. (2006). Why whyville? *Learning and Leading With Technology, 34*(6), 30–33.

Two
Science Learning Issue #2
Assessment

In Chapter 1, we explored how scientific inquiry might help improve science education learning outcomes. Further, we gave an example of how immersive environments could facilitate learning through scientific inquiry. But in order to enact any of those ideas, we need to think carefully about assessment. Learning and assessment are related cyclically. Assessments test what should be learned, while what is assessed impacts teaching and learning practices. This chapter focuses on this interdependency, but emphasizes that while our current assessment practices are driving instructional practices, best learning practices must drive assessment design.

The story of institutionalized assessment is a classic American success story of rags to riches. Just about 100 years ago, there were no standardized assessments and no psychological or intelligence tests at all. Yet, now, tests have gone from design and research to policy to widespread implementation. State tests are used to determine student readiness for high school graduation; SATs are used to indicate undergraduate potential; GREs and a whole host of similar tests are similarly used to predict graduate program success. Further, many careers, most notably medicine and law, and now even teaching in some states, have required career-entry exams. There is not another aspect of education that has made the leap so

34 **Science Learning Issue #2: Assessment**

successfully and fully from design to full-scale implementation in such a relatively short time.

Why? Why did testing become such a part of our education culture? While there is no doubt that government financial pressures were crucial, that only changes the question to why was that so acceptable to us? The education research literature is rife with reasons, explanations, and excuses, but there is no doubt that standardized tests appeal to our sense of industrialization and competitive equality. The American Revolution occurred against a cultural backdrop that social strata predicted success. If you were born to the upper class, you were worthy of running the country, businesses, and banks. What made the American Revolution such a global revolution is that it was premised on the idea that everyone had the right to govern and be successful, regardless of one's position in society. There are some who believe that industrialization was a crucial step toward our independence fight. Thus, one might conclude that industrialization and equal rights are embedded in our societal DNA.

So, what is the connection between our fight for independence/ industrialization and assessment? The connection stems from measurement. Running a factory has clear, measurable outcomes: production, sales, revenue, overhead, and so forth. One might debate how to analyze and interpret these measures, but the measures exist. This leads us to want all of our investments to have similar measures to assess success, and there is no doubt that from a local government perspective, our biggest investments are in schools. Unfortunately, schools are not factories. Education is a soft target: how do you know for sure when someone has learned something? How is that quantifiable? And, is the learning of some content even the 'product' of schools? Our country's success in

Science Learning Issue #2: Assessment   35

industrialization has made us want, and even expect, measurable, clearly interpretable outcomes. But, in education, we are still debating what to measure and how, even while we design assessments.

Let's unpack this in science education. As we indicated in Chapter 1, not everyone agrees on what should be taught in science, and how to teach it. Thus, one might wonder how we can discuss assessments until we agree on learning goals. Unfortunately, in nearly simultaneous paths, we are designing assessments even while we are trying to decide what should be taught. If we cannot agree on what to teach, and therefore on what the assessments should test, then debating how to assess this unknown learning is pointless; yet, that is what we are doing. This is in direct opposition to educational curriculum design processes, which dictate that teaching, learning, and assessment should be tightly connected: what students should learn drives what teachers should teach, and what tests should assess.

How should this play out? Learning goals drive both assessment design and teaching focus. Outcomes of assessment indicate how successful teaching was toward helping students achieve those learning goals, and can be used to evaluate teaching practices and create remedial plans. This is represented in Figure 2.1. *Learning goals* are at the top, as knowing what these are is the first step. Once they are known, they drive *teaching focus* and *assessment design*. *Assessment outcomes* assess teaching of the learning goals, and provide input on changes needed in teaching. These connections are all indicated by the arrows between the concepts. Please note that there is not a line connecting *assessment design* to *assessment outcomes*. Test design should not impact what a student's assessment outcomes are, although as we discuss later in this chapter, they often unfortunately

Science Learning Issue #2: Assessment

do. There is, however, an arrow connecting *assessment outcome* to *assessment design*. Evaluating assessment outcomes for any signs of bias in our outcomes is crucially important, and we can use that information to improve design.

The arrows in the diagram are the intended relationships, but connections in real life are not limited to those relationships. For example, our diagram does not show an arrow between *assessment design* and *teaching focus*, but that connection does exist in practice. As shown in the diagram, both *assessment design* and *teaching focus* are connected through *learning goals*. In essence, they should cover the same thing, so a direct connection between them ought to be unnecessary. Even so, it is important to recognize that with our current societal pressures on high stakes testing, 'teaching to the test,'

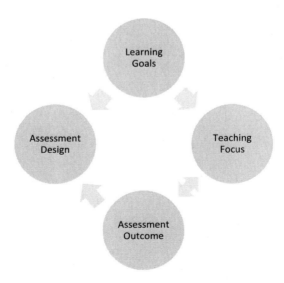

Figure 2.1 The Relationship between Learning, Teaching, and Assessment

Science Learning Issue #2: Assessment 37

that is, an arrow between *assessment design* and *teaching focus*, has unsurprisingly become the norm. While this term is often used derogatorily, teaching to the test is appropriate IF what students should learn is comprehensively covered on the tests as is implied in the preceding diagram should be the case. In other words, make an awesome test based fully on learning goals, and it does not matter if *teaching focus* is centered on *learning goals* or *assessment* as they are one and the same. Of course, the key here is to *make an awesome test!* As might be inferred, that is something that is far easier said than done, as we will explain throughout this chapter.

To summarize in general, when we think about how to design an assessment, we need to consider two factors: how comprehensively the learning goals are assessed, and whether the test design assesses those goals appropriately and without bias. For science education in particular, there are issues that stem from both of these crucial factors, and the factors themselves are tightly intertwined. As we indicated at the end of Chapter 1, assessment must complement the learning goals, and when it does not, assessment blocks growth toward our learning goals, especially if there is a cultural emphasis on teaching to the test. We discuss these issues in the rest of this chapter.

COMPREHENSIVE ASSESSMENT OF SCIENCE LEARNING GOALS

We identified the importance of learning goals driving assessment design. How does this play out in a traditional curriculum design process? Large learning goals are identified first. From there, grade and course learning goals are derived, followed by unit plans and ultimately lesson plans. Assessment is the last designed piece, because it relies on

38   Science Learning Issue #2: Assessment

the determination of what is being taught and learned. Most teachers go through this at a micro level each year. They take various district or state determinations of what information their students must learn, and then, they create a plan for how best to teach that (or they follow a specific curriculum guide designed by a curriculum team at their school from the state determinations). As they teach each unit, they create and administer formative assessments, assessments for progress checks, to see how well their students are learning that piece, and what might need modification. At the end of each unit, they design summative assessments, assessments for grading, to check the success of both their lesson plans and their students' learning. Again, the process starts with learning goals and ends with assessments, and this follows at a class level that we outlined in general in Figure 2.1.

Importantly, when teachers are designing their own assessments, they can vary the format, emphasis, and content being tested based on what they see is happening in the classroom. However, when tests are standardized, they must rely on a generalized set of standards during their creation. They must presume that all classrooms in a district, state, or nation are learning that same content, in the same order, and with the same emphasis. From one perspective, this seems like a good plan, because it will follow the curriculum design plan we set out earlier, with standards/goals leading to assessments. However, it misses all the middle steps of that design process, which we highlight here in italics: course goals ◊ *unit plans* ◊ *lesson plans* ◊ assessments. Instead, this is course goals ◊ assessments. With standardized tests, we no longer have the mediation of how the content is organized or taught.

So, why is that problematic? If assessment designers are not in contact with classrooms, then they must rely solely on

Science Learning Issue #2: Assessment   39

standards. But standards are typically lists of content, and do not take into consideration the interconnections between content topics that play out in the classroom. Let's take an example from the prior National Science Education Standards (NSES)[1] on which most of today's science assessments are still based. The NSES devoted a significant piece of the report's initial overview chapters to discussing the importance of scientific inquiry, and how inquiry should be integrated throughout the curriculum. The message was not unlike our message in Chapter 1: scientific inquiry is a crucial element of science education, and the curriculum should integrate content and inquiry. Unfortunately, after these initial overview chapters, the rest of the document was a listing of standards to guide actual practice, and included a single section on 'science as inquiry.' This sat side by side with sections for standards for physical science, life science, and five other categories. Thus, the organization of the standards themselves lost the crucial connection between content and inquiry, and instead, indicated that inquiry teaching and learning should take up one-eighth the class time and thus one-eighth the assessment space. Teachers in planning their lessons (or curriculum guides) would have taken into account the recommendation in the initial sections, but did assessment designers? According to a 2005 NRC report,[2] the answer is no. That report indicated that assessments designed from these standards created stand-alone questions for each of those eight categories, totally missing the vital connection between, as Dewey[3] phrased it, the practice of scientists and the outcomes of science practice, or in other words, scientific inquiry and science content.

Not only does that not connect to what good practice should be in the classroom, it has the insidious effect of implying that scientific inquiry is a thing on its own, no more

40 Science Learning Issue #2: Assessment

connected to life science, for example, than physical science is. We spent much of Chapter 1 indicating the crucial role of scientific inquiry in helping students learn about science and scientific practice. By doing so, we allow students to connect their prior learning to classroom learning, and increase their understanding of science. However, all this is undone if assessments treat scientific inquiry like a content and not a scientific practice. Assessments need to comprehensively assess science as it should be learned and taught, or they risk being an invalid measure of learning. This, then, is the keystone: tests must assess the range of what should be learned, or they risk becoming our implicit set of standards, overruling the stated standards themselves. This is why we state that while teaching to the test in an ideal assessment world is not an issue, it is a huge issue in our imperfect assessment world.

Clearly, this was partially a fault of the prior NSES. As we indicated in Chapter 1, the current standards, Next Generation Science Standards (NGSS),[4] have attempted to address this issue by suggesting that science instruction cover three main categories: science and engineering practices (encompassing what used to be called scientific inquiry), disciplinary core ideas, and crosscutting concepts interwoven in each lesson. While these standards are still written in some ways as separate sections, each page shows how the three categories should/could be integrated within a lesson.

NGSS is based on the four strands of what should be taught and learned in the *Taking Science to School* report that we discussed in Chapter 1. Therefore, we will continue to use the four strands in the National Research Council report, *Taking Science to School*,[5] as our guideposts of what is important to learn, teach and thus, assess. To refresh, that report outlined four categories of knowledge that students need to understand to be

Science Learning Issue #2: Assessment 41

'proficient in science.' The NGSS standards come from these four, and therefore, comprehensively outline what students should be learning in the science classroom:

1. Know, use, and interpret scientific explanations of the natural world
2. Generate and evaluate scientific evidence and explanations
3. Understand the nature and development of scientific knowledge
4. Participate productively in scientific practices and discourse.[5]

Are we then assessing all four of these strands? Tests need to assess all four categories outlined in the *Taking Science to School* report to be comprehensive measures of what should be learned in the classroom. Unfortunately, the current testing system in the United States focuses heavily on assessing knowledge and interpretation to the detriment of other aspects. A 2009 Carnegie Foundation report concludes:

> the need to obtain reliable results from tests that are easy and inexpensive to administer has driven assessments— and instruction—toward the first strand [of the *Taking Science to School* report's four categories] . . . and away from the other three more complex and difficult-to-assess competencies.[6]

Or, to put this in terms of NGSS, we have become adept at assessing disciplinary core ideas, but our current stable of assessments is less competent at assessing practices and conceptual understanding. To be sure, that report came out before the detailed NGSS, but only time will tell if this new standards

42   Science Learning Issue #2: Assessment

format has the desired outcome of making assessments more in consonance with good classroom teaching practice as we outlined in Chapter 1. Unfortunately, part of what drives this problem are other factors beyond how the standards are written, and we unpack those in the next sections.

THE IMPACT OF TEST DESIGN

One of the reasons our current tests are focusing on a subset of our science learning goals is due to the format of these tests itself. Assessing scientific inquiry and other deep concepts requires careful thought about design to avoid, as we stated earlier, the issue of assessment design directly affecting what is tested or how well students perform. Unfortunately, our current stable of district, state, and even national tests fails in this regard. The design of our current tests minimizes our ability to assess conceptual understanding, includes false positives, suffers from a lack of context, and has equity issues that render results for many invalid. We unpack each of these issues next.

Difficulty in Assessing Conceptual Understanding

We have already made it clear earlier in this chapter that we feel current assessments designed at the district, state, or national level are not assessing science comprehensively. One reason for this is that these tests rely on a multiple choice format for many reasons, not least of which is ease of administration and efficiency of grading. Unfortunately, this format is not well suited for assessing conceptual understanding and higher order thinking skills such as scientific inquiry.[7, 8, 9] We will illustrate this problem by exploring how scientific inquiry has been assessed in the past. Looking at the 2001 revision of Bloom's Taxonomy,[10] a classic hierarchy of learning, the upper

Science Learning Issue #2: Assessment

levels of the taxonomy represent most of what constitutes scientific inquiry as we have been discussing. As indicated in Figure 2.2, aspects of scientific inquiry, including designing, investigating, and experimenting, are found in the upper three levels of the taxonomy. However, one analysis of past K–12 science assessments indicated that students were more often assessed on the lower two levels of the taxonomy, asking students to identify or define aspects of scientific inquiry such as 'hypothesis' or 'control.'[2] This treats scientific inquiry as a content area, not as the key constituent in real science we believe it should be.

Unfortunately, this is having a direct impact on what is taught in the classroom, and is one of the reasons so little scientific inquiry is conducted in the classroom. In Chapter 1, we indicated several reasons for the consistent lack of implementation of scientific inquiry in the classroom. We left one of the key reasons for this problem to this chapter: the design of assessments. We stated that if assessments are

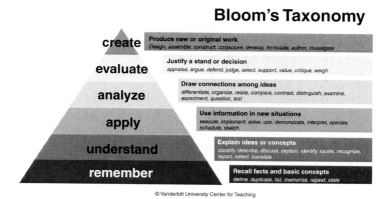

Figure 2.2 Revised Bloom's Taxonomy[11]

44 Science Learning Issue #2: Assessment

designed to assess science comprehensively, then teaching to the test would be fine, but in this case, the lack of real scientific inquiry, not just the focus on vocabulary, in assessments is having a major effect on practice. Falk and Drayton[12] studied the impact of instituting a high-stakes test in Massachusetts on six middle schools. They found that one school completely abandoned scientific inquiry in an attempt to meet the test content. Four were still committed to inquiry but felt that they had to broaden the topics taught and, therefore, give up some of their inquiry projects. The sixth school had never adopted inquiry and so made no changes.[13] These schools saw the science tests as being so focused on content to the point of requiring a change to their curriculum. The conclusion? If tests are going to drive instruction, then multiple choice questions as the primary, indeed sole in many cases, choice for assessment design needs to be reconsidered. Without better attention to this problem and given the positive relationship between engaging in scientific inquiry and increased conceptual understanding, this negative impact of tests on scientific inquiry in the classroom is not only alarming, but has the unintended consequence of ultimately lowering science conceptual understanding.

Let's be clear: this problem is not one of poor teacher practice, but rather a consequence of assessment design. Changing practice to fit a content-strong assessment is in some ways the mark of a teacher fulfilling job expectations. One of these job expectations is to prepare their students to pass a high stakes test, as the system continually makes clear to them through the various student and teacher accountability systems in place. Therefore, the issue that teaching to the test results in a loss of scientific inquiry in the classroom is instead the fault of a system that has created these incomplete high stakes tests

Science Learning Issue #2: Assessment   45

as a measure of student success and teacher quality. Imagine we are in a shoe factory where efficiency evaluators decided that to simplify their assessment of success they would only measure how many left shoes were created. We might presume that the evaluators thought that there was no need to measure both right and left shoes, because every pair to be sold would have one of each, or maybe they were functioning under such severe time and cost constraints that they felt this was the best method available to them. Of course, our presumptions might be completely wrong and the evaluators might have just been bad evaluators. In any case, if the measure of success of this factory line was how many left shoes it produced, it is not a stretch to see that over time to increase productivity and evaluation scores, more and more left shoes would be produced until few even remembered how to make a right shoe. When the CEO would then compare the factory success measures with the bottom profit line, is it any wonder that one would be high while the other low?

This relates directly to science education. We can focus our energies on raising test scores on incomplete measures of how much students have learned in school. However, not unlike our shoe factory, we then should not be surprised if unassessed knowledge decreases. If that unassessed knowledge is of minor importance, then there is little concern. However, if like in our shoe factory, the unassessed knowledge has significant long-term impact, then this becomes a substantial problem. Where does the case of scientific inquiry fall on this spectrum? Hopefully, we so successfully made our case in Chapter 1 about the importance of that unassessed knowledge that you, our reader, might already be anticipating our prognostications from this loss of a subset of our learning goals. Scientific inquiry is so strongly connected with

46 Science Learning Issue #2: Assessment

understanding and engagement that we worry that we are in danger of creating a citizenry with little interest in science, without a strong conceptual science understanding, and with a decrease in the creativity we used to be known for even in those that might become scientists. Indeed, we think we are already doing so.

As a solution, that same Carnegie report[6] recommends that a broad spectrum of assessments be utilized in science education, including performance assessments, portfolios, formative assessment, and high stakes assessments. These alternate forms of assessments increase the breadth of what can be assessed, and have a much better track record of assessing understanding at the upper levels of Bloom's Taxonomy. Some research indicates that performance assessments can show a higher level of understanding of content and process than do stand-alone multiple choice tests, especially for students in the bottom half of the class.[14] Thus, by broadening our approaches to assessment, we mitigate the issues of assessing conceptual understanding inherent in multiple choice questions.

Unfortunately, even this broad spectrum of assessments has difficulties associated with it. While alternative assessments, such as performance assessments and portfolios, are typically seen as capturing student understanding better than standardized tests, they are not cost-effective, cannot be compared from teacher to teacher, and some question their validity.[15,16] This issue is one of the reasons that high stakes tests rely on formats that have higher validity (evidence that what the test says it is measuring is indeed what it is measuring) and reliability (multiple testing yields the same result). Thus, we are caught between a rock and a hard place: we have tests with

Science Learning Issue #2: Assessment   47

demonstrated reliability and validity but with weak abilities to measure conceptual learning and scientific inquiry, and other assessments with questionable validity and reliability but strengths in assessing conceptual understanding and scientific inquiry. Logically, it would appear that neither format in isolation can give a full picture of student understanding. At the end of this chapter we will discuss a middle ground: computer-based performance assessments that demonstrate reliability and validity in assessing conceptual understanding and scientific inquiry.

False Positives

A second issue with the format of these tests is that of false positives. A false positive is when a test shows something exists that does not. In this case, we are applying this term to an educational assessment outcome that indicates a child has successfully learned a concept or fact when in fact they have not. How would that occur? Let's illustrate this with the case of understanding scientific inquiry.

We have indicated that many tests in the past have assessed scientific inquiry through multiple choice questions focused on definitions of words such as hypothesis. A student who memorizes this definition might have been characterized as someone who understands scientific inquiry. But is that accurate? Is knowing the definition of this word indicative of someone who can conduct an investigation, analyze data, and communicate findings? These are some of the characteristics we identified earlier as evidence of scientific inquiry. While it is possible that the two are linked for some students, it would be a difficult argument to sell that those skills and understandings are completely connected.

48 Science Learning Issue #2: Assessment

There is some evidence that supports the idea that false positives exist. For example, Michael[17] indicates that some students can take and pass science tests, but often are not able to indicate understanding of the concepts. Further, depending on how well-designed a multiple choice question is, the options can be indicative of the right answer. In practicing for an SAT many years ago, one of us (Ketelhut) decided to see how well I could guess. I answered every single question on the SAT, but marked the ones for which I was totally guessing. I then graded this practice test two ways: with the guessed questions all included and with none of them included. Even accounting for the then scoring process of subtracting for wrong answers, I discovered that my overall SAT score would be nearly 200 points higher if I guessed! Clearly, this is a completely anecdotal example, and one might argue not worthy of scientific consideration; nonetheless, it suggests that there are clues embedded in questions that can create a perception of understanding. The Carnegie Foundation's recommendation for a stable of assessments would help mitigate this, as there would be some triangulation between the outcomes of the various assessments to give a fuller and possibly more accurate picture of what someone knows.

There is also the reverse issue of false negatives. Teachers are familiar with the student who day in and day out performs at the top of the class, only to underperform significantly on multiple choice tests at the end of the unit. As former teachers, that was one of the most frustrating aspects of our practice, and is possibly related to test anxiety. There is another type of false negatives, caused by assessment design not anxiety, that is related to the lack of context in multiple choice questions. We discuss this and the inherent equity issues related to it in the next section.

Science Learning Issue #2: Assessment   49

Lack of Context

The third issue with assessment design relates to the importance of context, and is based in ideas of situated theory.[18,19] Situated theory hypothesizes that learning is contextual, and happens best when that context is close to that in which learning will be used. This is what we talked about in Chapter 1, when we discussed the value of immersive technologies as helping students feel as if they are in the real world, conducting authentic scientific inquiry. In those cases, learning was happening in a simulated context that mimicked the real one in which the learning might be used.

While many researchers have investigated the impact of designing learning around situated theory, matching assessments to the theory have been more problematic. We know it is important to match assessment to learning,[20] so if authentic contexts are key for learning,[21] then they might also have a strong impact on assessment. However, on a typical test, the material is usually isolated from the context in which it was learned or would ultimately be used;[22] it is hard to replicate authentic scientific contexts in the classroom and even harder to do so on a test, particularly on a text-based test. For example, assessing epidemiological inquiry skills in an authentic context would require students to engage with a real epidemic in a real environment, clearly not a viable option for large-scale assessment, or for that matter even appropriate to expose schoolchildren to a real epidemic.

Let's take an example from a released real test question to show the difficulties inherent in a context-less test question.[23] Suppose a test question is assessing student understanding of adaptation. An adaptation is a specific aspect of a living organism that provides a function associated with the lifestyle of that organism. To illustrate, a skunk's ability to spray a noxious

50 Science Learning Issue #2: Assessment

liquid is an adaptation that helps protect the skunk from predators. In this case, the test question is trying to ascertain if the student understands that stripes on a fish are an adaptation that helps protect it from being seen by predators. This question indicates in text the context: the fish lives in a muddy, weed-filled pond. As seemingly inconsequential as that phrase is, it is the key clue to solving this question. The student needs to know that weeds in a muddy pond are typically attached to the ground, and float straight up. A fish adapted to live in this environment has vertical stripes that blend into the weeds, thus protecting it from predators. In this case, anyone who has seen a muddy pond and understands the concept of adaptation would have no problem with solving this question. But, what about those students who understand adaptation but have never seen a muddy pond? Would they easily know what weeds do in such a pond? They might possibly be able to figure it out through their knowledge of adaptation and through a process of elimination of the possible answer choices, but not necessarily. Thus regardless of the outcome, this question is differentially difficult based on students' experiences in the world.

Earlier we mentioned that assessments need to show validity which we defined as evidence that what they say they are measuring is what they actually are measuring. False positives that we discussed earlier are potentially evidence against validity. Another aspect to validity is that the only thing that should differ between those that get a question right and those that do not is if they do not understand the concept being tested. If that's not the case, then, the test might not be measuring what it says it is measuring (e.g., adaptation), but instead some unknown quantity—a case of one kind of false negatives, mentioned earlier. If there is something about the

Science Learning Issue #2: Assessment   51

test that makes it harder for one group versus another, then we need to question the validity of that test. This example of the striped fish is nearly a classic definition of a validity issue. Unfortunately, the text-based format of many multiple choice tests often results in this specific type of validity issue, due to the inability of words to sufficiently indicate important contextual clues.

This concept of situated context is particularly problematic for students who do not have opportunities for a breadth of experiences to draw on when answering questions. Take, for example, the situation in many urban schools that have high percentages of poor and low socioeconomic status (SES) children. These children are rarely well traveled; indeed, many students do not leave their small neighborhood community within that city to even travel to another one within the same city! For these students, test questions like the fish example not only require them to try and apply what they have learned, but also to do so in isolation of any helpful mental images of places and things referred to in the text of the question. For example, many schools have district-wide tests that go by many names—benchmark, achievement, and so forth. We did a quick review of questions on a district-wide science test for a single grade in one large urban school district. We found that in one year, 20% of the questions referred to animals that would not be easily seen or experienced in an urban setting, not even at the local zoo; others referred to locations such as Europe or Florida, which for these students was no more familiar than questions about the moon. While knowing information about the animals and places is not crucial to success in those questions, these students cannot connect to even the little context given in the question, making the question that much harder to interpret and engage with,

52   Science Learning Issue #2: Assessment

as we described for the fish example. Only one question in all the tests reviewed actually referred explicitly to an urban context. This alone makes assessments more or less 'foreign' for different groups of students, leading to at best a more or less engaged student, and at worst a student without an equal opportunity. This is exactly why we did not draw an arrow in our Figure 2.1 to connect *assessment design* to *assessment outcomes*. These kinds of issues lead to bias in our tests which we discuss more later.

Equity Concerns

We have already begun to discuss equity concerns with the current set of standardized tests in the last section. Any test that is seen as more or less difficult because of where someone lives or what experiences that person has had is discriminatory.

As this issue became more obvious, some assessments attempted to account for the differences in contextual knowledge and experiences by creating open-ended questions that included all the information a test taker might need to know, regardless of their personal experiences. If we go back to the fish question, we could rewrite that question in a way that fit what these redesigners were doing. Instead of saying the fish lives in a muddy, weed-filled pond, we might instead say that the fish lives in a pond—that this pond is foggy because of all the mud that is in the water—that it is filled with weeds and these weeds are attached to the bottom of the pond and float straight up. After we do all of that, we can go back to ask the student about the fish and its adaptations. Instead of relying on a student's own personal context knowledge, that knowledge has been replaced by detailed, albeit lengthy text, sometimes with diagrams to lower the text need, but not always.

Science Learning Issue #2: Assessment   53

This solution, while inelegant, does help mitigate the problem of differential contextual knowledge in students. Unfortunately, the reliance of this solution on text for context adds its own problem: these lengthy questions rely on students' reading abilities as well as their science knowledge. A small study based on the TIMSS (Trends in International Mathematics and Science Study) assessment was conducted to explore this issue. The authors found that students could correctly answer science questions in a verbal interview that they had answered incorrectly on the test. The authors conjecture that poor reading and English language skills are partially to blame.[24] This study raises the question whether tests are assessing science knowledge, reading ability, or both. As we indicated earlier, this is a concern about validity for TIMSS test and others.

We have therefore identified two biases in our current tests that raise questions about whether all students are receiving accurate information about their *science* knowledge. Students without access to broad experiences and students with challenges in reading or English language might show up on our assessment outcomes as lacking *science* knowledge, when in fact what they are lacking are other forms of knowledge. This issue is a very serious one, as it means that some pockets of students are less likely to get accurate knowledge about their science abilities and thus have some possible science career paths closed to them due to non-science reasons. It is possibly behind the inequitable narrowing of the science pipeline.

A SCIENCE ASSESSMENT FRAMEWORK

To summarize, the issues with our current high stakes assessments are that they do not assess scientific inquiry or conceptual understanding well, and that they are dependent

54 Science Learning Issue #2: Assessment

on text, which is typically context-free or requires good English verbal skills. How do we then design a strong science assessment? One of us (Ketelhut) offers a framework for designing a good science assessment with five components: integration of scientific inquiry with content, contextualization with minimal reliance on text, efficiency of grading, statistical reliability and validity, and last, but definitely not least, engaging. This framework, nicknamed ICESE, incorporates all the ideas we have presented in this chapter.[25]

Traditional multiple choice assessments that we have discussed to this point show high marks for efficiency of grading and moderate marks for statistical reliability and validity, given some of the equity issues we have outlined. However, these tests rarely integrate assessment of scientific inquiry with content or contextualize their questions. Plus, we do not think that anyone would argue that these tests are the least bit engaging! While engagement might not seem to matter at first glance, on a deeper investigation, it is clear that if students do not apply themselves or struggle through difficult questions, then we will never know how well they have learned a concept. Therefore, getting students to stay focused and engaged is highly important.

If we consider other forms of assessments, as suggested by the Carnegie Foundation, we find a different set of successes and failures. For example, traditional performance assessments such as portfolios have strengths in contextualization and usually engagement as well. While they too often only assess a subset of content, creating a diverse set of assessments, which includes performance and multiple choice, can potentially assess most, if not all, of our learning goals. However, as we indicated earlier in this chapter, performance assessments as we have traditionally conceived of them suffer

Science Learning Issue #2: Assessment 55

from a lack of statistical validity and reliability. What is missing is a form of performance assessment without validity and reliability issues.

HOW CAN TECHNOLOGY HELP RESOLVE THIS ISSUE?

We have presented a framework for determining if a science assessment is designed in a way that will assess all of our learning goals without bias, and have indicated that traditional tests fail on some subset of these indicators. The question then is, can technology provide an alternative assessment route that succeeds on more or even all of these five design characteristics? The answer is not simple.

There is no doubt that technology can offer new insights into student understanding.[26] Many forms of interactive technology incorporate a database that records all student utterances and interactions that take place within the environment. For example, hypermedia consists of a series of information spaces that the user negotiates by activating links that take him or her from one space to another. The user can choose a relatively linear pathway through the spaces; or, if he or she so chooses, the pathway can be much more complex. Analyses of databases underlying hypermedia that record the features of these learner paths have illuminated student purposes and strategies while navigating the learning process.[27–29] Therefore, along with traditional and alternative assessments, this action data could enrich our perceptions of student understanding.

ICESE

In Chapter 1, we talked about the benefits of immersive environments to improve student conceptual understanding in science. If you recall, we indicated that using these

56 Science Learning Issue #2: Assessment

environments allows for potentially more 'real science' in K–12 science education, as they can overcome some of the obstacles toward classroom-based scientific inquiry. Since one of the issues with our current set of assessments is the lack of substantive scientific inquiry questions, a number of designers and researchers are exploring if this again is a place that these immersive environments can help.

Let's apply the ICESE framework to assessments based in immersive environments and see how they add up. First, the issue of assessing scientific inquiry with content—the I in our ICESE framework. We have already discussed in Chapter 1 that immersive environments are a perfect home for scientific inquiry learning, but can they also help us assess scientific inquiry or conceptual understanding more deeply than multiple choice questions? For this issue, the preponderance of evidence is indicating that yes, they can. Research indicates that using these virtual authentic environments for assessment creates an information stream that can be analyzed to give details about student problem-solving approaches which can be connected to both conceptual and process understanding.[26, 30] Further, the information in the databases underlying these environments give more information than just the 'right answer.'[31] Students do not only indicate what they think is the right answer, but the database holds evidence of the work they do to come up with the right answer. This can mitigate the false positives discussed earlier.

One of the issues with current assessments comes with the issue of context as we discussed at length earlier. This, of course, is one of the clear strengths of any visual media: its ability to situate the problem in an authentic context for students to solve. Immersive technologies among other formats allow for virtual recreation of scientists' labs and other

Science Learning Issue #2: Assessment 57

'real' contexts, thus obviating the need for reliance on student experiences. Further, visual media with less text than traditional assessment minimizes the impact of differential reading skills and English language abilities. The graphics provide visual clues to understanding words that might be unclear, not unlike the 'whole language' approach to learning to read. So, check for C = contextualized, and check for helping to address issues of equity!

What is still unclear, however, about these assessments is how efficiently they can be graded, and how statistically reliable and valid they are. The evidence is still accumulating, and at this time while not 100% clear, the trend is to showing positive steps toward achieving all of this.[32] So, the jury is still out on E and S of our ICESE framework.

There is little question that these are some of the most engaging tests we have seen to date. Most students tend to forget when 'playing the game' that they are also taking a test. We have seen students finish the test, and then opt back in to play some more. We are pretty sure that no one has opted to take the SAT a second time for fun!

The Example of SAVE Science

Let's explore a project that one of us (Ketelhut) has been leading with a team of collaborators for 8 years to illustrate what we have described here about using immersive environments for assessment. SAVE science, Situated Assessment using Virtual Environments for Science Content and Inquiry, was a project designed to investigate the use of immersive virtual environments (IVEs) for assessing science learning.[25] An immersive virtual environment, Scientopolis, was developed to assess middle school children's understanding of both scientific inquiry and science conceptual understanding.

58 Science Learning Issue #2: Assessment

Four assessment quests within Scientopolis (Figures 2.3 and 2.4) were created to elicit what middle school students have learned in their classroom, and were specifically designed to target standards that are currently poorly assessed on district or state assessments, as indicated by published success rates. In particular, the four topics and modules were: structure-function relationships ('Sheep Trouble'), weather fronts ('Weather Trouble'), gas laws ('Basketball'), and force and motion ('Two Rivers'). Students had an overall goal of uncovering the likely contributors to a problem facing a small virtual town or community (sick farm animals, weather-related crop failure, differently bouncing basketballs, and an injured researcher needing to reach a medic, respectively). Participants completed the modules by interacting with characters and objects in the IVE, collecting and analyzing clues, and using their existing understanding of both content and scientific inquiry to draw inferences—the I of the ICESE framework. Students could solve the problems in multiple ways.

To support grading and allow statistical analysis (the E and S of the framework) of the assessments, student activity was automatically recorded in the database with a location and time stamp. This allowed analysis of both explicit answers to questions posed by characters as well as students' processes in coming to those answers. Algorithms were created from this rich dataset to identify students on a continuum of understanding, and to give grade reports to teachers.

Our results over the years indicated that these assessments were feasible to design and analyze, and gave insight into student understanding in a way that typical assessments did not. Further, evidence toward reliability and validity was possible to develop, albeit not easily configured. But, in many ways, the strength of these modules was in their immersiveness and context, which supported some students to show

Science Learning Issue #2: Assessment 59

Figure 2.3 Scientopolis

Figure 2.4 Tool Use in SAVE Science

understanding where other methods had not, not unlike that TIMSS study mentioned earlier.[33] Indeed, in one small SAVE Science study, 22% of the students had been previously identified as not understanding the concepts being assessed based on a district-wide multiple choice test, but in the contextualized format of the immersive environment, these same students showed through their actions and ultimate solutions that they had indeed learned that content successfully.

Sadly, these and other students like them are being told in some cases that they have not learned the material, when in

60 Science Learning Issue #2: Assessment

fact they have. For these children, the lack of context has crucially impaired their ability to show what they really know. Therefore, they go through school thinking they cannot learn science, and many of them eventually opt out of trying to do so. Providing students with both traditional multiple choice questions and ones embedded in a format such as an IVE could permit a larger set of students to convey the real level of their science understanding. This could potentially open up science career pathways to a whole new set of students. Furthermore, overwhelmingly, students perceive this testing format to be more fun, less stressful, and a better way to evaluate more than just memorized knowledge.

SUMMARY

Concern abounds about the impact that current science assessments have on curriculum and instruction as teachers teach to tests that do not fully assess science. Most troubling of the issues with current assessments is their inequity, particularly around English language learning and experiential knowledge. While options such as the typical performance assessment alternatives could address some of the concerns, they are not feasible for large samples, such as urban districts or state-wide tests. Technology-based performance assessments, such as virtual environments, might provide an alternative to begin to solve some of the issues around standardization of performance assessments. Seeing this across the nation regularly in school districts is most likely still in the future, however.

REFERENCES

1. National Research Council. (1996). *National science education standards: Observe, interact, change, learn.* Washington, DC: National Academies Press.

Science Learning Issue #2: Assessment 61

2. National Research Council. (2005). *America's lab report: Investigations in high school science.* Washington, DC: National Academies Press.

3. Dewey, J. *Democracy and education* (First free press paperback 1966 ed.). New York: Palgrave Macmillan.

4. NGSS Lead States. (2013). *Next generation science standards: For states, by states.* Washington, DC: National Academies Press. Retrieved from www.nextgenscience.org/next-generation-science-standards

5. National Research Council. (2007). *Taking science to school: Learning and teaching science in grades K-8* (Committee on Science Learning, Kindergarten Through Eighth Grade, R. A. Duschl, H. A. Schweingruber, & A. W. Shouse, Eds.). Board on Science Education, Center for Education. Division of Behavioral and Social Sciences and Education. Washington, DC: National Academies Press (p. 2).

6. Carnegie Corporation. (2009). *The opportunity equation: Transforming mathematics and science education for citizenship and the global economy.* New York: Carnegie Corporation of New York (p. 28).

7. Mislevy, R., Chudowsky, N., Draney, K., Fried, R., Gaffney, T., & Haertel, G. (2003). *Design patterns for assessing science inquiry.* Menlo Park, CA: SRI International.

8. Southerland, S. A., Smith, L. K., Sowell, S. P., & Kittleson, J. M. (2007). Resisting unlearning: Understanding science education's response to the United States' national accountability movement. *Review of Research in Education, 31*, 45–77.

9. Resnick, L. B., & Resnick, D. P. (1992). Assessing the thinking curriculum: New tools for educational reform. In B. Gifford & M. O'Connor (Eds.), *Changing assessments: Alternative views of aptitude, achievement, and instruction* (pp. 37–75). Norwell, MA: Kluwer Academic.

10. Anderson, L. W., & Krathwohl, D. R. (2001). *A taxonomy for learning, teaching, and assessing: A revision of Bloom's taxonomy of educational objectives.* New York: Longman.

11. Vanderbilt University Center for Teaching. (2016, September 6). *Bloom's taxonomy.* Retrieved from https://cft.vanderbilt.edu/guides-sub-pages/blooms-taxonomy/

12. Falk, J., & Drayton, B. (2004). State testing and inquiry-based science: Are they complementary or competing reforms? *Journal of Educational Change, 5*, 345–387.

13. Nelson, B., & Ketelhut, D. J. (2007). Scientific inquiry in multi-user virtual environments. *Educational Psychology Review, 19*(3), 265–283.

62 Science Learning Issue #2: Assessment

14. Ketelhut, D. J., Dede, C., Clarke, J., & Nelson, B. (2007). Studying situated learning in a multi-user virtual environment. In E. Baker, J. Dickieson, W. Wulfeck, & H. O'Neil (Eds.), *Assessment of problem solving using simulations* (pp. 37–58). Mahwah, NJ: Lawrence Erlbaum Associates.

15. Stecher, B. M., & Klein, S. P. (1997). The cost of science performance assessments in large-scale testing programs. *Educational Evaluation and Policy Analysis, 19*(1), 1–14.

16. National Research Council. (2001). *Knowing what students know: The science and design of educational assessment.* Committee on the Foundations of Assessment. In J. Pelligrino, N. Chudowsky, & R. Glaser (Eds.). Board on Testing and Assessment, Center for Education. Division of Behavioral and Social Sciences and Education. Washington, DC: National Academies Press.

17. Michael, J. (2007). Conceptual assessment in the biological sciences: A National Science Foundation sponsored workshop. *Advances in Physiological Education, 31,* 389–391.

18. Brown, J. S., Collins, A., & Duguid, P. (1989). Situated cognition and the culture of learning. *Educational Researcher, 18,* 32–42.

19. Lave, J., & Wenger, E. (1991). *Situated learning: Legitimate peripheral participation.* New York: Cambridge University Press.

20. Krajcik, J. S., McNeil, K. L., & Reiser, B. J. (2007). Learning-Goals-Driven design model: Developing curriculum materials that align with national standards and incorporate project-based pedagogy. *Science Education, 92*(1), 1–32.

21. Steele, M. (2005). Teaching science to middle school students with learning problems. *Science Scope,* 50–51.

22. Behrens, J.T., Frezzo, D., Mislevy, R., Kroopnick, M., & Wise, D. (2007). Structural, functional, and semiotic symmetries in simulation-based games and assessments. In E. Baker, J. Dickieson, W. Wulfeck, & H. O'Neil (Eds.), *Assessment of problem solving using simulations.* New York: Lawrence Erlbaum Associates.

23. The Commonwealth of Pennsylvania. (2011). *Pennsylvania system of state assessment.* Retrieved February 2011, from www.portal.state.pa.us/portal/server.pt/community/pennsylvania_system_of_school_assessment_(pssa)/8757/resource_materials/507610

24. Harlow, A., & Jones, A. (2004). Why students answer TIMSS science test items the way they do. *Research in Science Education, 34,* 221–238.

Science Learning Issue #2: Assessment   63

25. Ketelhut, D. J., Nelson, B., Schifter, C. C., & Kim, Y. (2013). Improving science assessments by situating them in a virtual environment. *Education Sciences*, 3(2), 172–192.

26. Ketelhut, D. J. (2007). The impact of student self-efficacy on scientific inquiry skills: An exploratory investigation in River City, a multiuser virtual environment. *Journal of Science Education and Technology*, 16(1), 99–111.

27. Barab, S., Bowdish, B. E., & Lawless, K. A. (1997). Hypermedia navigation: Profiles of hypermedia users. *Educational Technology Research & Development*, 45(3), 23–41.

28. Barab, S., Bowdish, B. E., Young, M. F., & Owen, S. V. (1996). Understanding Kiosk navigation: Using log files to capture hypermedia searches. *Instructional Science*, 24(5), 377–395.

29. Marchionini, G. (1989). Information-seeking strategies of novices using a full-text electronic encyclopedia. *Journal of the American Society for Information Science*, 40(1), 54–66.

30. Baker, E., Niemi, D., & Chung, G. K. W. K. (2007). Simulations and the transfer of problem-solving. In E. Baker, J. Dickieson, W. Wulfeck, & H. O'Neil (Eds.), *Assessment of problem solving using simulations* (pp. 1–18). New York: Lawrence Erlbaum Associates.

31. Nelson, B., Ketelhut, D. J., Schifter, C., Sil, A., Slack, K., & Kim, Y. (2014, November 6). *Featured research—Basketball trouble: A game-based assessment of science inquiry and content knowledge.* Featured paper presented at the Association for Educational Communications and Technology Annual Meeting, Jacksonville, Florida.

32. Gobert, J. D., Kim, Y. J., Sao Pedro, M., Kennedy, M., & Betts, C. (2015). Using educational data mining to assess students' skills at designing and conducting experiments within a complex systems microworld. *Thinking Skills and Creativity*, 18, 81–90.

33. Ketelhut, D. J., & Shelton, A. (2012). Using immersive virtual environments to assess science understanding: The impact of contextualization. In P. Felicia (Ed.), *Proceedings of the 6th European Conference on games based learning* (pp. 235–241). Reading, England: ACI.

Three
Science Learning Issue #3
Motivation

In Chapter 1, we focused on issues in learning science, particularly what we called 'real science.' To reinforce our concerns about the current state of the practice, we started the chapter with a quote from the well-known Bruce Alberts about his view of the current issues in science teaching. That quote is also a good place to start this chapter on exploring issues related to motivation. To refresh, Bruce Alberts said:

> Those of us who are passionate about science have thus far failed to get real science taught . . . that difficult concepts are taught too early in the science curriculum, and they are taught with an overly strict attention to rules, procedure, and rote memorization . . . when we teach children about aspects of science that the vast majority of them cannot yet grasp, then we have wasted valuable educational resources and produced nothing of lasting value. Perhaps less obvious, but to me at least as important, is the fact that we take all the enjoyment out of science when we do so . . . Tragically, we have managed to simultaneously trivialize and complicate science education. As a result, for far too many, science seems a game of recalling boring, incomprehensible facts.[1]

The point that Alberts is making is a crucial one. Our current approach to science education is sending the message to

Science Learning Issue #3: Motivation 65

children that science is boring, fact-based, and incomprehensible. For a few lucky ones (Diane is one of those!), informal science education and parental involvement turn boring science into a world of wonder. That's the world that Alberts wants all children to experience, not just those born into it.

Motivation is hugely important in learning and assessment. We have hinted at this throughout the first half of this book. We cannot force children to learn anything, but we can make them want to learn it. Far too often, motivation is ignored or placed on the back burner by policymakers and science curriculum designers. It is not an uncommon refrain to hear someone suggest that it is all well and good if they *like* what they are doing in school, but did they *learn* anything? Undoubtedly, learning is the primary goal of education, but this refrain implies that learning and motivation are distinct from each other, that you can have learning regardless of whether there is motivation. In fact, learning and motivation are tightly connected. Consider one of your own hobbies. Have you ever tried to teach a friend about that hobby and had their eyes glaze over part way through your passionate lesson? One of us is a sports nut, and has learned to hide that fact from many friends. No matter how we share what makes our team important to us and fun to follow, our non-sports friends just do not understand it. The same is true for education. No matter how well or how passionately you teach a topic, if your audience is uninterested, unengaged, or feeling as if there is no way they can do it, your lesson will fail. No learning will happen. Thus, motivation is the linchpin to successful learning.

Later we unpack three aspects that we feel are important to improving science understanding from the perspective of motivation: self-efficacy, interest (including career interest), and growth mindset. We recognize that trying to unpack these

66 **Science Learning Issue #3: Motivation**

aspects individually is at best artificial. These aspects are tightly woven together, and we have already introduced aspects of them briefly in the previous chapters because it is so very difficult to pull them apart. That said, in this chapter we will discuss the importance of each, the issue surrounding them related to science education, and then explore how learning technologies might play a role in mitigating the issues.

SELF-EFFICACY

In seminal work, Bandura[2] defined self-efficacy as the belief that one can successfully perform certain behaviors. For example, in the science classroom, a student might be asked to do a science fair project. In this situation, a student's self-efficacy refers to their sense that they can perform the tasks that are involved in conducting a science fair project. For some, this engenders excitement; for others, this is a moment of dread. While there is more than one reason for the disparity, it in part stems from a difference in a self-perception that one can do the work, that is, self-efficacy for science fair projects. Often, these students who dread it will say, "I'm not a science student."

But, does this really matter? Or, is this a case of as long as they are learning, should anyone care? Further, pertinent to this book, is this really a science education issue that needs to be included, or rather just an indication of the diversity of students? Of course, not all students are meant to be Einsteins, and some might be more on track to be Picassos, so why should we care whether all students think of themselves as capable of being 'science students'? We cannot state strongly enough how crucial we think it is that we DO care, and how this is unequivocally an important science education issue!

Science Learning Issue #3: Motivation   67

We started this book talking about the alarming state of science knowledge in the general population on topics that affect each and every one of us, such as the general ignorance in the public of the differences between viruses and bacteria. Whether students plan to be artists or scientists, we need each of them to become a science-educated adult, who is capable of making evidence-based decisions on important topics, such as antibiotics, that affect us all. Since, as we said at the start of this chapter, motivational aspects like self-efficacy are tightly tied to success in the science classroom for all students, we need each child to become self-efficacious in science.

What do we know about the impact of self-efficacy in the classroom that underlies our belief in its importance? Self-efficacy is tied to a student's behavior in the classroom so that their ability to learn is impacted, particularly their ability to comprehend complex ideas, such as those of evolution or scientific inquiry. For example, Pajares[3, 4] argued that self-efficacy affects behavior by regulating an individual's choices, the extent of his or her expended effort, and his or her emotional responses. Thus, in the classroom, students with higher self-efficacy are more likely to: persevere in difficult situations;[4, 5] see complexity as a challenge;[4] be engaged;[4] see failure as indication that more effort is needed;[5, 6] choose specific strategies to enhance learning;[7] and attribute success to their own efforts.[3] Students with lower self-efficacy are more likely to see complexity as an insurmountable obstacle, equate failure to bad luck and poor innate ability,[3, 4] and presume that a problem is more complex than it is and thus not worth attempting.[4] This is not about who should be a scientist, but much like our argument for scientific inquiry in the classroom, it is instead about creating the best learning

68 Science Learning Issue #3: Motivation

opportunities for all students. The literature is clear that self-efficacy levels have a strong impact on achievement.[8–11]

We want all students to be engaged, to see problems as a challenge not an obstacle, and to attribute their success to their own activities not to luck. Thus, we want all students to develop a strong sense of self-efficacy. This is what makes for successful learning. Consequentially, we want all students to be in learning environments that will then help them develop that strong sense of self-efficacy for that learning activity. Luckily, self-efficacy levels are not fixed, are related to specific aspects/topics, and are impacted by what we do in the classroom. So, if we agree that to maximize learning we need to maximize a student's perceived self-efficacy, then, that is something we can definitely impact in the science classroom.

Let's explore very briefly how this might happen. Bandura[2] outlined four sources for how someone develops their sense of self-efficacy. First and most powerfully, someone's own experiences impact their self-efficacy. Positive, successful experiences raise self-efficacy, whereas negative, unsuccessful ones lower it. So, in our earlier example of doing a science fair project, a student might have raised their self-efficacy based on prior successful experiences in doing what is required for a science fair project. Second, vicarious experiences can similarly impact self-efficacy. For our science fair project example, a student might see his peers successfully conducting the tasks of a science fair project and thus feel more self-efficacious that they too can do it. Third, verbal persuasion may have an impact, such as a teacher encouraging the student to persevere on their science fair project. Finally, a person's emotional feedback can have an impact. So, in our science fair project example, a student feeling tension or stress over accomplishing

Science Learning Issue #3: Motivation   69

the included tasks of the project might develop a decrease in self-efficacy for those tasks.

Every time a student enters the classroom, all four of these sources of self-efficacy are in play. Each experience by the student or their peers, each interaction with the teacher, and each negative emotional state have an impact. So, imagine a student who has been successful in the science classroom and hangs out with other successful students. This student most likely walks into each experience in the science classroom with high expectations and high confidence of accomplishment. In contrast, imagine a student who is unfamiliar with success in the science classroom, and works with other students of similar experiences. This student likely has low self-efficacy in science with little opportunities to improve it. It is not hard to see how self-efficacy might explain some of the behaviors and outcomes in our science classroom. Nor is it difficult to understand the dichotomy that results in students seeing themselves as into science or not a science student.

What makes self-efficacy an important issue specifically for science education is that we see a precipitous decline across the school years. The National Assessment of Educational Progress[12] included a question measuring self-efficacy, which asked students to rate the phrase: "All can do well in science if they try." Eighty-two percent of fourth graders agreed with this statement; however, only 64% of eighth graders and a mere 44% of twelfth graders agreed. While self-efficacy researchers agree that some decline in self-efficacy levels is expected as we mature and become more realistic about our abilities, this steep decline is alarming. If self-efficacy is strongly related to behaviors in the classroom that are themselves related to learning, then we need to find a way to improve or maintain

70 Science Learning Issue #3: Motivation

higher self-efficacy levels as children go through their science courses.

How to do that? Of all of the sources of self-efficacy, the most powerful is personal experiences, what are sometimes called mastery experiences. There are many ways to help students achieve a positive mastery experience, but in the science classroom, scientific inquiry is the most effective for a number of reasons. First, we know that self-efficacy is a context-specific attribute, even in seemingly overlapping contexts. For example, a student might hold a high self-efficacy for acting but a very low one for reading, even though acting often requires reading scripts. So, in the science classroom, if we attempt to raise self-efficacy in a specific domain—such as biology or chemistry—we would need to attack each of these separately. But scientific inquiry experiences might offer a comprehensive backdoor. Research seems to indicate that there can be a generalizability of self-efficacy if students see the same skills used in different domains. [13] In that case, levels of self-efficacy might extend to multiple areas. So, imagine a student who has had positive experiences while conducting scientific inquiry investigations on plant growth, thus positively impacting his self-efficacy for scientific inquiry and possibly for plant biology. This student is then asked to conduct a scientific inquiry project in a new topic such as how electric circuits work. The student might feel more confident about his ability to learn about electrical circuits than he might have otherwise, because of his confidence in conducting scientific inquiry.

A second reason that scientific inquiry is a good way to positively impact self-efficacy is intrinsic to the process of scientific inquiry. As we discussed in Chapter 1, scientific inquiry engages students in pursuing understanding. As a

Science Learning Issue #3: Motivation   71

result, students have a higher potential of having mastery experiences, as well as vicarious ones, since much of scientific inquiry is done through group work in the classroom. It is much easier for a student to mentally or physically withdraw from participation in teacher-centered pedagogies than from student-centered ones. Supporting this idea, it has been shown that undergraduates who participate in research experiences have higher science self-efficacy than those who do not.[14]

There is another critically important aspect to focusing on raising self-efficacy in formal science classrooms from kindergarten on up. As we stated in the beginning of this chapter, some students are raised in homes that promote positive science experiences. These students begin formal schooling with a higher self-efficacy for science than others who have not had that advantage. Let us repeat this: at the beginning of schooling, students enter with diverse levels of perceived self-efficacy. Thus, from day 1, given the impact of self-efficacy on learning behaviors, some students will be more engaged, try harder, and use better metacognitive learning strategies than others.[4–7] Classrooms that focus on providing positive mastery experiences give *all* students the opportunity to develop high self-efficacy and thus positive learning behaviors. However, if classrooms look like the ones that Alberts decried earlier—boring and overly complex—then students without science experiences outside school will quickly disengage, and never have the chance to develop their science self-efficacy. Because informal science experiences often rely on resources that some families do not have access to, this becomes an equity issue that schools have the potential to impact. Sadly, this potential, as we have discussed in prior chapters, is not always realized.

72 Science Learning Issue #3: Motivation

INTEREST INCLUDING CAREER INTEREST

There has been much discussion about the narrowing pipeline in science, from the perspective of both cause and solution. A number of well-publicized documents have drawn attention to this problem nationwide with varying frames of reference: business, research, development, and so forth.[15–17] But, the bottom line is that we interest far too few students (hence the narrowing pipeline analogy) in scientific careers, and that narrowing starts early. One-third of all high school students only take a single year of science; 82% of high school seniors fail to reach proficiency in science on the National Assessment of Educational Progress (NAEP). The students represented by these related statistics have closed the door to a future in science before they even reach college.

While no one disputes that the pipeline is narrowing, there are those who do not see that as a problem. After all, we do not want everyone to major in science or become a scientist! What does seem indisputable and troubling, however, is that the narrowing is not equitable. The pipeline seems to be differentially narrowing for women and minorities, resulting in the outflow of that pipeline not reflecting the composition of the United States.[17] If we consider the pipeline to start at kindergarten and go through to post-college careers, then, there are multiple decision points related to science, such as picking high school electives, choosing a college and then a science-related college major, completing a major in science, and pursuing a graduate degree in science. At each major decision point, we see the percent of women and non-Asian minorities who choose science decreasing relative to the whole group.[18] For example, according to the U.S. census in 2011, while the U.S. population was nearly 50% women, women represented only 26% of those in STEM careers.[19] There is no doubt we

Science Learning Issue #3: Motivation   73

have made strides in the last 50 years or so in retaining more underrepresented minorities and women, however, there is also no doubt that we have a long way to go.

How does this situation happen? Students begin school with a basic interest in science as evinced by their natural tendency to ask 'why' questions, as any parent knows. However, this interest seems to wane across K–12, until many are left without an interest in science, and indeed without even remembering their early childhood fascination with how the world works. As a result, many only take the bare minimum required science courses in high school, which often limits their choices of college and major down the road. Tai, Liu, Maltese, and Fan[20] found a strong correlation between eighth graders who wanted a science career and those that graduated with a college degree in science. Thus, this narrowing of the pipeline is set in place as early as middle school.

There is some indication that this narrowing of interest by some specific subpopulations is happening in middle school. For example, gender differences begin to be seen by the beginning of middle school. Jensen and McMullen[21] investigated when gender differences in science interest first appear. They found that students attending a gifted and talented summer institute program showed no gender differences in career interest in science at the fifth grade level, but gender differences in science career interest appeared by sixth grade. Further, their interest in a scientific career was significantly correlated with their desire to take more science classes in high school, which as we have indicated often forms a gateway to higher education in science and thus careers. Other studies reinforce the importance of middle school for science interest by pointing to data showing racial and SES differences in science interest by the end of middle school. One study

74 Science Learning Issue #3: Motivation

classified eighth and ninth grade students into four groups by interest: *science is me* through to *science is not me*.[22] Sadly, slightly over half of the students were in the *science is not me* group, but even more significant is that this group was overly represented by low SES students. Waiting until high school to try and impact interest in science appears to be too late.

Clearly, not only are we losing a large percentage of students before they have had a chance to experience much science, but we are losing them differentially based on SES, gender, and race/ethnicity. Luckily, research indicates several factors that are associated with increasing students' career interest in science. First, students with higher self-efficacy (we did say that these topics were connected!) are more likely to pursue a career in that field.[23] Second, students who participate in scientific inquiry, whether in formal or informal learning environments, appear to improve their interest in science as a career.[24, 25] Thus, you can see that we have not overestimated the importance of scientific inquiry in the first chapter of this book. It is the thread that connects most of the issues we are focusing on. While we do not mean to harp on it, however, you will recall from Chapter 1 that we have stated that one of the major issues in science education is the lack of consistent and authentic scientific inquiry in the classroom. The ramifications of this keep growing.

GROWTH MINDSET

Another important factor in student success in *real science* classes is the degree to which they believe that ability is not a fixed trait. That is, do they believe that ability and intelligence can be changed over time with hard work? This belief is called an *incremental theory of ability*,[26] or more commonly, a *growth mindset*. Imagine two students tasked with collecting data from a

Science Learning Issue #3: Motivation   75

local pond as part of an ecosystem unit. The first student has a high *growth mindset*, while her classmate does not, sometimes called a *fixed mindset*. The two students must first identify areas of the pond that are likely to be habitats for large fish, and then, use sensors attached to their phones to monitor water temperature and pH. Both students initially struggle to identify the appropriate areas to sample, but the first believes more strongly that she can learn the complex process. In the end, she persists and completes the task, while her classmate disengages at the first sign of failure, and ultimately learns less from the task. While mindsets can vary across a spectrum of fixed to growth, this hypothetical example indicates the impact this belief has on success.

Having a growth mindset has been shown to be an important predictor of academic success. Students who have a growth mindset are more likely to view failure as a normal part of learning, to view effort as a way to meet goals, persist when faced with difficulties, and ultimately demonstrate higher achievement levels than their peers with fixed mindsets.[27] In addition, students with growth mindsets are more likely to draw on many different sources to frame their belief that they can achieve, while those with fixed mindsets tend to focus on negative psychological states (e.g., anxiety and stress) to inform these beliefs.[28] Given the importance of fostering a growth mindset, you might ask "how can I do this in my own science classroom?"

There are many ways that teachers and curricular designers can structure curricula and lessons to support growth mindsets in their students. For example, in one study, college students in one group were asked to imagine themselves after they had learned content. They wrote about potential obstacles to learning, established goals to reach their desired level

76 Science Learning Issue #3: Motivation

of learning, and described how they would reach their goals. Their peers in another group were not asked to do any of these things. At the end of the study, those student who had set incremental goals, and envisioned themselves as having learned via those goals, demonstrated more learning gains and were more likely to take full course loads the following semester.[29, 30] In essence, the key to successfully supporting a growth mindset is to structure the curriculum so that students can set goals and learn the content *incrementally*, and to praise students' *effort* and not their intelligence (which hints at a fixed intelligence that cannot change as students learn).[31] If we go back to our science fair project example from earlier in this chapter, we could envision that project being set up in stages to allow students to achieve each piece along the way. It is not hard to understand, however, why so many children have difficulties with science fair projects because they are far too often set up with one large goal of a presentation at the science fair. For those struggling to attain a growth mindset, this global goal could be daunting.

It should also be noted that there are various structural components to public education that act to suppress students' beliefs that they can achieve over time, such as high-stakes testing, tracking, and high student-teacher ratios.[32] While classroom teachers cannot do much to change these structures, they can be aware that they may act against their efforts to foster growth mindsets in their students. This put an even larger emphasis on designing classroom experiences that allow students to grow.

Having a growth mindset is clearly related to success in doing, and learning, *real science*. Of particular importance are the abilities to persist when struggling to learn. For example, how to identify relevant data, how to use that data to update

Science Learning Issue #3: Motivation 77

mental models, and how to change goals is an important aspect of science, especially as inquiry-based tasks become challenging and complex. In the brief example at the top of this section, the student who believed that she *could* learn the skills and knowledge required to complete the unit was ultimately successful, and likely learned more from the activity. These supposed connections are supported by recent research, as well. Different studies have shown that science students who believe that failure is a part of learning, and that failing when they tried complex tasks did not mean they were incapable of learning (a central component of having a *growth mindset*), were more highly motivated and demonstrated more learning.[33, 34] In our experience as former science teachers, students were commonly heard to ask if they had the right answer. It was difficult to convince them that science grows whether the 'answer' is what was expected or not.

This research is not without critics, however, although the body of research supporting it is growing. And, as with the other constructs discussed in this chapter, there are connections between students having a growth mindset, their interest, and their self-efficacy. In fact, research has shown that students with more strongly pronounced growth mindsets have higher interest in science and science self-efficacy![35] This makes sense, because belief that you can do the work required (self-efficacy) is a prerequisite to believing that you can learn, given that you do the required work (growth mindset), and both of these beliefs are likely to motivate interest in science.

HOW CAN TECHNOLOGY HELP RESOLVE THIS ISSUE?

Motivation is definitely an area that technology can play a strong supportive role. One only has to observe what children do as soon as they are 'released' from school to see the

78 Science Learning Issue #3: Motivation

potential for technology. When I (Ketelhut) was little, TV was just exploring its potential. There was one show on Saturday morning that I would not miss. You were told to put a piece of clear plastic over the TV screen, and at certain points in the story, the character would ask for the viewer's help in solving some problem, such as drawing a bridge over a chasm to allow the hero to escape the villain. The engagement of being interactive with the story was without compare then. Today's computer games are in many ways just a more sophisticated version of that TV show from my childhood. But, most importantly, research on immersive environments designed to be like computer games indicates that these environments positively impact all three aspects of motivation that we have talked about in this chapter: self-efficacy, interest, and growth mindset.[35–37]

We talked in Chapter 1 about the immersive virtual environment, River City. We can use River City as one example for how these environments can impact our three aspects of motivation. Let's start with self-efficacy. We know that self-efficacy levels are impacted by mastery experiences,[2, 6] and participating in a game-like environment engages participants in a series of activities, designed to be mastered by everyone. Therefore, we would expect to see students with low self-efficacy gradually improve their self-efficacy as they progress through these levels. This effect can be seen in research conducted with River City and other similar environments.[37, 38] For example, in River City, as students progressed through the levels, the differences in their initial interactions with the curriculum that could be correlated with their self-efficacy levels completely disappeared part way through.[37] Initially, students with low self-efficacy interacted with the environment far less than those with higher self-efficacy. Less interaction means less learning. But, over time, all students interacted with the

Science Learning Issue #3: Motivation   79

curriculum at the same level as those who had started with high self-efficacy. In other words, the immersive environment evened the playing field of learning.

We also see a powerful effect on student interest. Just like that Saturday morning TV show, immersive environments like computer games are built around a story line, and as we talked in Chapter 1, they immerse the user in that story line. That immersion can have a beneficial impact on career interest, depending on the design. For example, the *River City* environment was designed to put the student in the role of a scientist. For possibly the first time in their lives, students took on the identity of an expert in science, and spent two weeks behaving as a scientist. What was the outcome of this? Students told us over and over again how they felt like a scientist for the first time. Further, even though surveys on career interest for preteens and early teens are often too general to show an impact, we found a small increase in interest in a career in science.[39]

The *River City* curriculum, and other curricula like it that are built around immersive environments, allow students to monitor their progress, receive feedback at critical points, and provide opportunities to try new strategies in a low-stakes environment. For example, students in *River City* could see if the experiments they chose to conduct resulted in reduced numbers of mosquitos, which were an important vector for disease transmission in the virtual world. If not, they could try another experiment and check results again. These supports have been shown to support students in developing a growth mindset.[40]

SUMMARY

Motivation is a critical aspect of authentic science learning. The aspects of motivation we highlight in this chapter—self-efficacy, interest, and growth mindset—are not only individually important, but they are tightly related to one another as well as to

80 Science Learning Issue #3: Motivation

learning. As educational technologies become more ubiquitous, curricula should focus on leveraging these motivational factors to support learning.

REFERENCES

1. Alberts, B. (1995). Panel urges shift of focus for school science courses. *Science.*
2. Bandura, A. (1977). Self-efficacy: Toward a unifying theory of behavioral change. *Psychological Review, 84*(2), 191–215.
3. Pajares, F. (1995). *Self-efficacy in academic settings.* Paper presented at the American Educational Research Association, San Francisco, CA.
4. Pajares, F. (2000). *Schooling in America: Myths, mixed messages, and good intentions* (Report). Cannon Chapel, GA: Emory University.
5. Lent, R. W., Brown, S. D., & Larkin, K. C. (1984). Relation of self-efficacy expectations to academic achievement and persistence. *Journal of Counseling Psychology, 31,* 356–362.
6. Bandura, A. (1986). *Social foundations of thought and action: A social cognitive theory.* Englewood Cliffs, NJ: Prentice Hall.
7. Zimmerman, B. J., & Bandura, A. (1994). Impact of self-regulatory influences on writing course attainment. *American Educational Research Journal, 31,* 845–862.
8. Pajares, F. (1996). *Assessing self-efficacy beliefs and academic outcomes: The case for specificity and correspondence.* Retrieved February 21, 2004, from www.emory.edu/EDUCATION/mfp/aera2.html
9. Stajkovic, A. D., & Luthans, F. (1998). Self-efficacy and work-related performance: A meta-analysis. *Psychological Bulletin, 124,* 240–261.
10. Wigfield, A., & Eccles, J. S. (2002). The development of competence beliefs, expectancies for success, and achievement values from childhood through adolescence. In A. Wigfield, & J. S. Eccles (Eds.), *Development of achievement motivation* (pp. 91–120). San Diego, CA: Academic Press.
11. Zimmerman, B. J. (2000). Self-efficacy: An essential motive to learn. *Contemporary Educational Psychology, 25*(1), 82–91.
12. National Center for Educational Statistics. (2000). *The nation's report card.* Retrieved October 12, 2003, from http://nces.ed.gov/nationsreportcard/

Science Learning Issue #3: Motivation   81

13. Schunk, D. H., Pajares, F., Wigfield, A., & Eccles, J. (2002). The development of academic self-efficacy. In A. Wigfield & J. Eccles (Eds.), *Development of achievement motivation.* San Diego, CA: Academic Press.

14. Berkes, E., & Hogrebe, M. (2007). *Undergraduate laboratory research, persistence in science, and the effect of self-efficacy beliefs: A quantitative study.* Chicago, IL: American Educational Research Association.

15. National Science Foundation. (2001). *Characteristics of doctoral scientists and engineers in the United States,* 2001 [Internet]. National Science Foundation. Retrieved March 19, 2004, from www.nsf.gov/sbe/srs/nsf03310/pdf/tab6.pdf

16. Grigg, W., Lauko, M., & Brockway, D. (2006). *The nation's report card: Science* 2005 (NCES 2006–466). U.S. Department of Education, National Center for Education Statistics. Washington, DC: U.S. Government Printing Office.

17. Committee on Prospering in the Global Economy of the 21st Century: An Agenda for American Science and Technology, National Academy of Sciences, National Academy of Engineering, Institute of Medicine. (2007). *Rising above the gathering storm: Energizing and employing America for a brighter economic future.* Washington, DC: National Academies Press.

18. Griffith, A. L. (2010). Persistence of women and minorities in STEM field majors: Is it the school that matters? *Economics of Education Review* 29(6): 911–922.

19. Landivar, L. C. (2013). *The relationship between science and engineering education and employment in STEM occupations,* ACS-23, U.S. Census Bureau. Retrieved June 19, 2017, from www.census.gov/prod/2013pubs/acs-23.pdf

20. Tai, R., Liu, C., Maltese, A., & Fan, X. (2006). CAREER CHOICE: Enhanced: Planning early for careers in science. *Science,* 312(5777), 1143–1144.

21. Jensen, R. A., & McMullen, D. (1995). A study of gender differences in the math and science career interests of gifted fifth and sixth graders. Washington, DC: U. S. Department of Education, Office of Educational Research and Improvement. (ERIC Document Reproduction Service No. ED 379 811.)

22. Aschbacher, P. R., Ing, M., & Tsai, S. (2014). Is science me? Exploring middle school students' STE-M career aspirations. *Journal of Science Education and Technology,* 23, 735–743.

82 Science Learning Issue #3: Motivation

23. Lopez, F. G., & Lent, R. W. (1992). Sources of mathematics self-efficacy in high school students. *Career Development Quarterly, 41*, 3–12.

24. Gibson, H., & Chase, C. (2002). Longitudinal impact of an inquiry-based science program on middle school students' attitudes toward science. *Science Education, 86*, 693–705.

25. Savage, L., Ketelhut, D. J., Varnum, S., & Stull, J. (2010, March 22). *Raising interest in science careers through informal after-school experiences.* Paper presented at the National Association for Research in Science Teaching, Philadelphia.

26. Dweck, C. S., & Leggett, E. L. (1988). A social-cognitive approach to motivation and personality. *Psychological Review, 95*(2), 256.

27. Dweck, C. S. (Ed.). (1999). *Self-theories: Their role in motivation, personality, and development.* Philadelphia: Psychology Press.

28. Chen, J. A., & Usher, E. L. (2013). Profiles of the sources of science self-efficacy. *Learning and Individual Differences, 24*, 11–21.

29. Morisano, D., Hirsh, J. B., Peterson, J. B., Shore, B., & Pihl, R. O. (2010). Setting, elaborating, and reflecting on personal goals improves academic performance. *Journal of Applied Psychology, 95*, 255–264.

30. Duckworth, A. L., Grant, H., Loew, B., Oettingen, G., & Gollwitzer, P. M. (in press). Self-regulation strategies improve self-discipline in adolescents: Benefits of mental contrasting and implementation intentions. *Educational Psychology.*

31. Mueller, C. M., & Dweck, C. S. (1998). Praise for intelligence can undermine children's motivation and performance. *Journal of Personality and Social Psychology, 75*(1), 33.

32. Grubbs, W. N., & Oakes, J. (2007). *Restoring value to the high school diploma: The rhetoric and practice of higher standards.* Boulder, CO: National Education Policy Center.

33. Harsh, J. A., Maltese, A. V., & Tai, R. H. (2011). Undergraduate research experiences from a longitudinal perspective. *Journal of College Science Teaching, 41*, 84–91.

34. Hernandez, P. R., Schultz, P. W., Estrada, M., Woodcock, A., & Chance, R. C. (in press). Sustaining optimal motivation: A longitudinal analysis of interventions to broaden participation of underrepresented students in STEM. *Journal of Educational Psychology.* https://doi.org/10.1037/a0029691

35. Chen, J. A., Metcalf, S. J., & Tutwiler, M. S. (2014). Motivation and beliefs about the nature of scientific knowledge within an immersive

Science Learning Issue #3: Motivation   83

virtual ecosystems environment. *Contemporary Educational Psychology*, 39(2), 112–123.

36. Meluso, A., Zheng, M., Spires, H., & Lester, J. (2012). Enhancing 5th graders' science content knowledge and self-efficacy through game-based learning. *Computers and Education*, 59, 497–504.

37. Ketelhut, D. J. (2007). The impact of student self-efficacy on scientific inquiry skills: An exploratory investigation in river city, a multi-user virtual environment. *Journal of Science Education and Technology*, 16(1), 99–111.

38. Bergey, B. W., Ketelhut, D. J., Liang, S., Natarajan, U., & Karakus, M. (2015). Scientific inquiry self-efficacy and video game self-efficacy as predictors and outcomes of middle school boys' and girls' performance in a science assessment in a virtual environment. *Journal of Science Education and Technology*, 24(5), 696–708.

39. Ketelhut, D. J., Nelson, B., Clarke, J., & Dede, C. (2010). A multi-user virtual environment for building higher order inquiry skills in science. *British Journal of Educational Technology*, 41(1), 56–68.

40. Kazakoff, E. (2017). *Cultivating a growth mindset with educational technology*. Retrieved March 9, 2017, from www.lexialearning.com

Four

Implementing Technologies Into Science Classrooms

In the preceding chapters, we explored three central issues in science education (learning 'real science,' assessment, and motivation), and have highlighted ways in which technologies can be used to help address each in turn. As most teachers who have tried will tell you, however, technology integration is no simple task. Identifying areas where technology might benefit student learning requires time for reflection and experimentation, which is often missing in a teacher's life. Once such areas are identified in a curriculum, structural, cultural, and institutional barriers often impede the employment of a novel technological solution. It's no wonder, then, that in a world inundated with constantly evolving technologies upon which we are growing increasingly more reliant, classrooms seem to lag behind as technology-enhanced spaces.

We often hear comparisons between classrooms and the world outside of education, with classrooms being referred to as old-fashioned at best. In a world where technology is ubiquitous and constantly innovating, classroom-based technologies are often outdated, outmoded, and in short supply. When they are available, these technologies are often relegated to a separate physical space, for example, computer labs, or are wheeled in on carts and shared by students. While these shared devices (usually notebooks or tablets) allow students to stay in their science classrooms, the lack of a dedicated device means students often have to re-install software or transfer files between uses. In both cases, learning is disrupted; technology is seen as added-on, not integrated into pedagogy. While we agree that these technology-based concerns are crucially important, we note that they have been addressed at length elsewhere.[1]

There is, we propose, another set of important implications and issues that we want to address when considering the integration of technology into science classrooms in particular. Namely, two central questions should drive this decision, and these questions connect to what we have written in prior chapters: (1) how does technology interact with the decision of *what* should be taught in science, and (2) in what ways do technologies support *how* important science concepts and skills are taught and assessed? In this chapter, we explore these questions and comment on how they interact with policy and the process of teacher education. We begin by describing the interaction of educational technologies and two components of classroom education: curricula and pedagogy, making policy recommendations as appropriate throughout. We next highlight research-based frameworks for supporting pre-service and in-service teachers in implementing technologies in pedagogically appropriate ways in order to support curricular goals. Finally, we provide some example frameworks for evaluating the success of technology integration efforts, before turning our attention to potential future trends in the integration of technologies in science education.

FACILITATING IMPLEMENTATION THROUGH CHANGES IN POLICY AND PRACTICE

When considering the implementation of technologies into science classrooms, we feel it is important to consider

86 Implementing Technologies

two overarching recommendations, which we develop next. *First, the technologies being introduced should support clear curricular goals.* We have discussed the importance of integrating learning of scientific practices with that of conceptual understanding, as well as how technologies, particularly immersive ones, can support this. Therefore, we stress the importance that these technology-supported curricular goals cut across specific curricular topics. *Second, teachers need to be supported in developing strong pedagogical methods for integrating technology into their classrooms.* Unfortunately, many teachers developed their own pedagogical understanding in a technology-lite environment, and thus need to be continually supported through professional development in connecting their pedagogical knowledge to include seamless technology integration.

Curriculum

Any successful implementation of technology into the classroom should flow from a coherent set of expectations (i.e., standards) for its optimal use by all members of an educational community. *Our first curricular proposal, then, is that this set of expectations or standards need to be adopted and implemented at the highest possible level of organizational administration.* We will talk later about the connected need to ensure that participants at all levels of the teaching and learning process are supported in successfully meeting the goals such standards set.

One particularly well-organized set of standards are those proposed by the International Society for Technology in Education (ISTE). The ISTE has sets of standards specifically for students, teachers, and administrators,[2] each of which clearly defines the knowledge and skills that educators and students need to develop in order to be ultimately successful in

Implementing Technologies 87

technology-rich workplaces. The student standards are concentrated around seven general goals that technologies can help students to achieve, and which students must master in order to be successful in the modern world. Students should develop into a(n):

1. Empowered learner
2. Digital citizen
3. Knowledge constructor
4. Innovative designer
5. Computational thinker
6. Creative communicator
7. Global collaborator.

The teacher standards, then, center on goals that help teachers hone and develop their own skills while helping students to reach the seven goals previously outlined. As a result, these standards are divided into what makes an 'empowered professional' and how to be a 'learning catalyst.' An empowered professional vis-à-vis technology is a:

1. Learner
2. Leader
3. Citizen

While, similar to the student standards, a learning catalyst is a(n):

4. Collaborator
5. Designer
6. Facilitator
7. Analyst.

88 Implementing Technologies

We have only listed the title of each of these standards. Each of these is broken down in a way that science teachers and administrators (or, district or state level leadership and instructional designers, as it were) can use them to set curricular goals to help ensure that students are receiving authentic and high-quality science education that is properly supported by, and that prepares students for success in our technology-rich world. Areas of overlap between the ISTE standards and prevailing science standards such as the NGSS abound. Let's unpack one of the ISTE student standards, *knowledge constructor*, as an example. A knowledge constructor according to the ISTE standards is a student that makes use of technologies for constructing learning and research opportunities, with a focus on evaluation and problem solving. A teacher who is a *leader* creates the environment for such learning. Finally, the NGSS[3] suggests that each lesson should include some aspect of their eight *science and engineering practices*. Three of these, asking questions, planning investigations, and analyzing data, connect directly to the ISTE standard, constructing learning and research opportunities, detailed earlier. Thus, the leader in technology standards, ISTE, integrates smoothly with the current set of science standards.

Unfortunately, this smooth integration runs into roadblocks. As we have indicated previously in this book, science teachers in K–12 schools are often given 'canned' curricula, including lab-based activities, and asked to enact them in lock-step with their peers over the course of the school year. This helps to ensure that students all receive the same amount of content over the same amount of time, and facilitates interpretation of the standardized tests that often happen at the end of the school year, which is ostensibly a good thing. Unfortunately, all too often curricula in schools is years-old.

Implementing Technologies 89

This is doubly problematic in science, because not only is the science not reflective of new understandings, but the suggested technologies can include those that seem as outdated as 8-track tapes! Further, the technologies in canned curricula are often add-ons or passive components of lessons, undoing all the benefits of technologies that we have been discussing in the previous chapters. However, policies that force teachers to rigidly adhere to the materials provided with the curricula may prevent them from finding and using current technologies that better support learning.

Given that we know that the choices that teachers make when enacting a technology-enhanced lesson plan may impact how their students learn, how can we support and empower those teachers to make optimal choices when the optimal choice might not be supported by the required curriculum? This leads to our second curricular proposal: teachers need to be engaged in the curriculum design and lesson planning processes. This gives them critical insight into why specific technologies are used, and how best to use them while empowering them to push for solutions to issues that they are the best situated to know. This proposal is supported by the ISTE teacher standards of empowered professional, which calls for teachers to be leaders in improving teaching and learning for students.

This is, of course, an ideal scenario. As former classroom teachers, we understand that the time and energy needed to undertake the design and implementation of a well-developed curriculum and related lessons can be daunting. Far too often, time and resource constraints cause technologies to sit idly in boxes or to be used on special days for enrichment only. Unfortunately, as Harvard University's Chris Dede[4] has succinctly put it, sidelining technology is akin to using it like

90 Implementing Technologies

fire, but, unfortunately while 'you can benefit from standing near a fire; you can't benefit from just the presence of a mobile device.' There are, however, examples of lesson-design paradigms that would allow teachers to identify critical points within a curriculum, and decide how best to use and integrate technologies into their practice.

One example that lends itself particularly well to this process is the Teaching for Understanding (TfU) framework.[5] Using TfU, educators can identify concepts or skills within a curriculum that are particularly important to understand, perhaps because they are foundational for future learning. The educators then state achievable goals that will help students focus on the critical aspects of the surfaced concepts or skills. Next, the educators design learning experiences that allow students to develop and demonstrate understandings of the stated goals. Finally, the educators use ongoing assessment information to give students feedback about their learning at critical points. Lesson planning, then, is a matter of providing students with a range of appropriate experiences to develop and demonstrate their understanding across manifold modalities.

Technology integration can be a critical part of every step of this process.[6] As we have stated throughout this book, concepts and skills that are important but difficult to understand can often be better learned with the help of technologies, such as visualization and simulation. As outlined in the example of immersive virtual environments (IVEs) throughout this book, the development and demonstration of understanding can then further be supported by technologies, including feedback to teachers and students. Frameworks such as TfU allow technologies to be used at the right time, with the right students, and in the right amount.

Implementing Technologies 91

Another approach to integrating technology into the curriculum can be through the process of Backwards Design[7] that is often taught in teacher education schools. In this process, teachers figure out the learning goals or outcomes before designing the actual experiences. If you remember back to Chapter 1, where we discussed a solid curriculum design process which starts with goals and ends with assessments, in many ways that is a form of Backwards Design. Knowing what the outcomes should be for students can help focus teachers on what technological experiences can best aid in achieving those results.

It is critical, then, that opportunities to learn technology-enhanced lesson planning using frameworks, such as TfU or Backwards Design, be a central part of teacher education and professional development. The concept of making teachers be a central part of curriculum and lesson design is not new. The matter was discussed 20 years ago by Ball and Cohen,[8] who concluded that teachers necessarily need to play a central role in design decisions. The issue is more critical now, however, as the promise and potential of technologies to enhance learning through instruction and assessment continue to expand.

Pedagogy

While the ISTE standards outline goals for student learning and teacher practice, how teachers implement them can be crucially important. Teachers in problem-based, technology-enhanced curricula curate the experience of students as they move through the virtual environments either in groups or individually. The decisions a teacher makes change the way her students interact with a given technology, and almost certainly impact what her students learn from the experience. Throughout our research, we

92 Implementing Technologies

have found teachers new to integrating student-centered technologies to fall into three categories: the Monitors, the Sages, and the Facilitators. The Monitors are the teachers who think that these environments are self-contained teaching units, needing little from the teacher beyond monitoring the classroom. The Sages include teachers who are more comfortable with teacher-centered practices, and thus are reluctant to implement these more student-centered experiences. These teachers tend to undermine the affordance of the technology to empower students by using them more as teacher-led demonstrations. Finally, the last group of teachers, the Facilitators, are the ones that implement technologies in the classroom in a way that supports the ISTE standards. They add to but do not subtract from the benefits of the technology. The goal is to move all teachers toward and into the Facilitator category.

The importance of doing this cannot be stressed enough. The role of the teacher can augment or diminish the benefits of immersive environments to solve the issues of science education that we have been discussing throughout this book. For example, Shari Metcalf and her colleagues at Harvard found that the degree to which teachers followed best practices of implementation (that is, to the degree to which they were Facilitators) was positively related to student content knowledge after using a science-based multi-user virtual environment (MUVE).[9] Similarly, one of us (Tutwiler) found that, compared to students with a different teacher, students with the same teacher tended to show similar patterns of interaction in a science-based MUVE. Students in a given class tended to collect the same types of data in the virtual world, over time.[10] This strongly suggests the likelihood that the different teachers were giving different types of guidance to the students over the course of the 2-week curriculum. In the first study, teacher practice impacted student learning, and in the second study, it impacted engagement with scientific inquiry. These studies hint at an obvious though important insight: the decisions that teachers make while facilitating a learning experience interact with the effect of technologies integrated into classrooms. Maximizing the positive effect of these technologies on learning and engagement goes beyond design decisions; it is crucial that teacher practice receive as much if not more attention.

In the preceding curriculum section, we highlighted the need to consider standards and models of curriculum development that will help teachers to effectively integrate technology into their classrooms. Thus, given the importance of how teachers are using these tools, the logical next step is to consider how best to execute lessons and use technologies in support of student learning. We approach this issue by first considering a theoretical framework that explores the types of knowledge needed to successfully integrate technology, and then highlight some best practices in professional development to support effective technology integration.

Multiple types of knowledge must be brought to bear when integrating technology into a curricular unit or lesson plan. Koehler and Mishra formalized this concept, and hypothesized that teachers must balance their understanding of content central to the curricular goals with their knowledge of pedagogical best practices and technology use, a framework they referred to as Technological Pedagogical Content Knowledge (TPACK).[11] We illustrate the TPACK framework in Figure 4.1.

94   **Implementing Technologies**

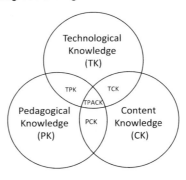

Figure 4.1 The TPACK Theoretical Framework

The constituent components of Figure 4.1 are knowledge about:[12]

- TK—the use of hardware and software
- PK—theories of learning and assessment
- CK—the subject matter (for our purposes, this is science knowledge)
- PCK—methods to aid in the learning of specific content (i.e., best practices for learning science in specific)
- TPK—methods of the use of technologies to aid in teaching and learning
- TCK—ways to use technology to research and report upon specific content (i.e., technology for science)
- TPACK—ways to use technology to aid in the teaching and learning of specific content (e.g. science)

For example, a chemistry teacher may have a certain level of knowledge in using wikis to research information about a given topic (TK), the best pedagogical practices for facilitating student-centered learning (PK), and hydrogen bonding

(CK). She will also, based on experience and study, know that she often has to use analogies when teaching about processes at the atomic level (PCK), the use of wikis as a curated collaborative space for student knowledge generation (TPK), and specific computer-based simulations that demonstrate hydrogen bonding (TCK). The convergence of all of these knowledge components is the teacher's TPACK. For this example, her TPACK is her knowledge that student learning will be maximized by integrating wikis and simulations into a student-centered, collaboration-based unit. In that unit, students will propose and test theories about hydrogen bonding based on their use of the simulation, and then construct and share evidence of their understanding through authoring their own wiki entries while peer-editing others' wiki entries.

It has, therefore, been proposed that TPACK should be introduced into the curricula of programs for pre-service teachers.[12] The degree to which novice teachers can reflect upon and address deficiencies in these various knowledge components is hypothesized to be directly related to the potential success of the integration of technologies into their classrooms. As highlighted in the review by Voot and colleagues,[13] this is commonly accomplished by engaging students in technology-rich lessons or involving them in modeling how to teach in a technology rich environment. Voot and colleagues also reviewed research on increasing in-service teachers' TPACK, usually via professional development, a topic toward which we now turn.

Much scholarship has been directed at defining, refining, and re-defining teacher professional development and how it is best conducted. One recent bit of research that we think captures the key components well was put forth by Desimone and Garet, who conceive of a five-feature definition of effective professional development:[14]

96 Implementing Technologies

1. Content focus—specifically, how students learn the content
2. Active learning—teachers engage in creating and evaluating example student work
3. Coherence—content of the professional development align with the curriculum and goals of the teachers
4. Sustained duration—20 hours or more of time on task
5. Collective participation—groups of teachers from similar cohorts (subject, school, etc.).

Building upon this model, and the degree to which we believe curricula and pedagogies interact with technology integration and TPACK, we recommend professional development aimed at fostering technology use in science classrooms be structured in ways similar to those described below.

1. *Start by having groups of educators who teach the same or similar subjects identify specific topics that are particularly difficult to teach, learn, or assess.* These topics are often disengaging to students, and are frequently the ones most likely to be served by some type of technology.[6]
2. *Give the teacher-teams time both to explore potential technological solutions to their identified topics, as well as to embed it in a sample lesson or lessons.* This will help to ensure that the solutions identified fall within the range of technological self-efficacy of the teacher.
3. *Have members of the teacher-teams take turns practicing with the technologies as both instructors and learners.* This will allow teachers to identify potential areas where misconceptions are likely to occur.
4. *Encourage members of each teacher-team to think of ways to evaluate the success of the technology in the given context.* Practice using these assessments informally during the PD.

Implementing Technologies   97

5. *Support teacher-teams to allow them both to observe each other implementing the technologies in the classroom and to reflect on the implementation afterwards.* Follow-through to actual practice is key in promoting use in the classroom.[15]

These are, of course, ideal conditions and expectations. In reality, technologies, not pedagogical needs, are often at the center of a given PD. For example, a school might hire a technology consultant to come teach about the use of Google Docs, Blogger, or various video games in their classrooms. In that scenario, the technology becomes the focal point, drawing attention away from the important aspects of Content and Coherence outlined earlier in the characteristics of effective professional development.[14] That is not to say that time should not be spent exploring the detailed intricacies of many given software packages. However, to the maximum extent possible, one should attempt to ensure that the professional development is tied to what teachers see as relevant and important topics. Remember back to the introduction to this book. We stated strongly that we take the stance of science education first, and technology second; in other words, the why before the what. We urge that same stance as much as possible in teacher professional development.

FRAMEWORKS FOR SUPPORTING AND EVALUATING TECHNOLOGY INTEGRATION

So far we've outlined ways to identify and integrate technologies into curricular units. We as teachers are familiar with ways to evaluate the effectiveness of traditional curricular materials by assessing student engagement and learning. Proper evaluation and iterative improvement to the integration of technologies is something that teachers and

98 Implementing Technologies

instructional designers know relatively less about, however. This is not a new problem. Frameworks for the evaluation of technology integration began to appear almost as soon as educators began using computers and other technologies in their classrooms. For example, over 20 years ago Christopher Moersch and colleagues developed a framework for measuring classroom technology use[16] that was itself derived from work conducted 20 years prior to their own.[17]

In this section, we will highlight three modern frameworks that can be used to help guide teachers in their own efforts to integrate technologies into their classrooms and evaluate how efficacious that integration was. These frameworks are complementary, attacking the issue of successful implementation at different points, from the initial creation of a receptive environment to how to implement. We then give a brief example of how they might be used jointly.

Individualized Inventory for Integrating Instructional Innovations (i⁵)

One critical step in technology integration is being able to identify potential barriers to the integration of a technological innovation into the classroom prior to the actual implementation. Groff and Mouza highlight six general categories into which such barriers might fall:[18]

1. Research and policy: Unclear research-based evidence and inconsistent policies
2. Technology: Malfunctioning technologies or network connectivity
3. Context (The School): Lack of resources or support for technology use

Implementing Technologies 99

4. Innovator (The Teacher): Inadequate technology skills or negative attitude toward technology
5. Innovation (The Project/Unit): Deviates from school culture or current practice
6. Operators (The Students): Expectations about and comfort with technology use.

As they point out, the first two line items, "Research and Policy" and "Technology," are largely out of the control of educators, while the remaining four items can be directly measured by teachers prior to engaging in a technology-rich curriculum or implementing a technology-enhanced learning environment.[18] The authors developed the Individualized Inventory for Integrating Instructional Innovations (i[5]) to help teachers identify potential traits of the Context, Innovator, Innovation, and Operators that may act as barriers, and to guide teachers in finding solutions.

Teachers are encouraged to use the i[5] in a two-step process. First, teachers rate the Context, Innovator, Innovation, and Climate each along three separate dimensions using the i[5] rubric available at https://sites.google.com/site/edtechi5/. For example, in the Context category the teacher would rate how supportive the teaching environment, technology staff, and technological infrastructure are. If a teacher notes that she is the only teacher who regularly uses technology, but that her school's technology staff is supportive and the school's technology infrastructure is well-maintained, she would focus her resources on enlisting other teachers to partake in the technology implementation with her, in order to maximize resources and help build a collaborative culture around this innovation.

100 Implementing Technologies

Substitution, Augmentation, Modification, and Redefinition (SAMR)

Once barriers to implementation have been identified, teachers require a framework that will allow them to track their progress as they integrate the given technology over time. Based on the previously discussed TPACK model, Ruben Puentedura's Substitution, Augmentation, Modification, and Redefinition (SAMR) framework allows teachers to identify at which stage of technology integration they currently operate, in order to help guide them to a higher-level integration as they iteratively refine their approach and gain the requisite skills.[19]

For example, a middle school science teacher, in an effort to help expose her students to the process of scientific collaboration, may choose to use a collaborative online platform, such as Google Docs, to allow her students to make notes and co-author a lab report. The first time the teacher uses this technology, she uses it strictly as a substitute for pen-and-paper science notebooks and word processor–based lab reports by having students type their observations directly into a 'science notebook' document, and then create a second document for their lab report. Both documents would them be handed in via email. The second time she uses it, however, she may explore other functionality of the platform, such as having students hyperlink their lab report to their observational science notebook document in order to cite specific evidence. In her third iteration of the technology-enhanced unit, our example teacher may ask her students to publish their lab reports online in order to share their work with their peers, and engage in a simulation of blind peer review as part of the evaluation process. Finally, the teacher may share her technology-enhanced unit with other teachers

Implementing Technologies 101

Table 4.1 Example of Stages in the SAMR Framework

Stage	Task
Substitution	Use the collaborative tool as a word processor to co-author two documents
Augmentation	Hyperlink between the documents
Modification	Engage classmates in peer review
Redefinition	Collaborate and engage in peer review with students outside of the class

online, and have her students work collaboratively and engage in peer review with students around the world. These last two iterations allows our science teacher to help students engage in one of NGSS's science and engineering practices: *obtaining, evaluating, and communicating information.*[3]

In this example, the teacher began by using the technology strictly as a *substitution* for what she had previously done. Next, she *augmented* the task by leveraging affordances unique to that technology. She then *modified* the curricular unit itself by using the technology to layer on the component of peer-review. Finally, she *redefined* the nature of the lesson itself by engaging in cross-cultural collaboration. So, not only did she evolve her use of the technology but by doing so, she evolved the science practices in her classroom which is our ultimate goal. We highlight this progression in Table 4.1, above.

Technology Immersion Model (TIM)

Although they focus on different aspects of the technology integration process, the i5 and SAMR frameworks both assume that the process of technology integration is gradual and largely directed at the classroom level. Depending on the climate of the school, however, this may not be the case in

102 **Implementing Technologies**

many instances. Top-down integration of multiple technologies (often driven by secular trends in technology use outside of educational environments) is not uncommon. For example, a school may install wireless internet routers, update their desktop, laptop, and tablet computers, and install suites of new educational and productivity software all in short order.

What supports are necessary for such an undertaking to be successful? One candidate framework for this type of implementation is the Texas Center for Educational Research Technology Immersion Model (TIM). The TIM calls for seven components for ideal top-down implementation:[20]

1. Leadership—principals have clear visions and expectations about technology integration and use
2. Teacher Support—teachers share their understanding about technology and have access to resources to help support the integration of technology
3. Parent and Community Support—parents and the community understand and support technology integration
4. Technical Support—local staff help troubleshoot barriers to implementation
5. Professional Development—teachers receive adequate and ongoing professional development
6. Classroom Immersion—technology is used to change teaching practice and support higher order learning and skills
7. Student Access and Use—students have access to and use technology at school and home.

To give an example, imagine that you work in a school that has applied for and been awarded a substantial grant to allow for a systematic overhaul of your school's technology

Implementing Technologies 103

infrastructure. Using the TIM as a guide, you can help facilitate working groups of teachers and administrators to identify areas in which your school might be adequately strong, and others that need improvement in order to be successful.

As mentioned earlier, these three frameworks can also be used jointly to both determine how to initiate a technological transformation as well as evaluate how successful prior initiatives were. For example, if your school is planning a top-down technology initiative, you may use the TIM framework to determine whether previous technology initiatives have changed teaching practice or been otherwise transformative in the past (Classroom Immersion), and whether students have had regular access to those educational technologies (Student Access and Use). If you find that previous initiatives have not transformed teaching and learning, you might then employ the SAMR model to identify how technologies have been used in the past in order to understand why prior implementations were unsuccessful. Determining that the technologies were used entirely for Substitution and Augmentation of older tools would indicate a need in this new venture to engage teachers in professional development directed toward moving them away from the lower levels of SAMR and toward the upper ones of Modification and Redefinition. In addition, you might ask all of the teachers to complete an i^5 rubric in order to gauge perceived barriers to the newly planned technologies in the integration, and identify ways to address them.

SUMMARY

In this chapter, we explored various factors that work together to impact the use of technologies in science classrooms. These concepts are closely related, of course, and we close with an example of how they might all work together in a hypothetical

104 **Implementing Technologies**

scenario in which a teacher intends to use a specific technological tool to help support student learning.

Mariana works in a school that has just been awarded a sizeable grant to update its technological infrastructure, and support the use of technology in the classroom. Her administration adopts the ISTE standards, and uses the TIM model to help guide the integration process. They have set up a series of professional development workshops to allow teachers to share their expertise and identify areas where technology might best support learning. During the science teacher workshop Mariana's group completes a TPACK survey to assess the degree to which various members of her department feel comfortable using technology to teach specific science content. She then meets with her peers and brainstorms to identify concepts that have historically been difficult for her students to understand. Her group lands on two topics: atomic structure and scientific modeling. She and her peers then explore various technological options that might help students understand why scientists use models to represent complex and difficult-to-observe systems and processes, one of which is the 'atom.' The group thinks that these areas may benefit from some type of simulation or enhanced demonstration to better promote learning.

After finding a host of simulations of experiments that resulted in the formulation of increasingly more complex models, she and her peers coordinate to build a curricular unit that allows students to replicate these classic experiments while making observations about and comparing the models that each supports. Curriculum in hand, her science department completes an i^5 inventory to assess expertise and support. After identifying which colleagues might need extra support, the department facilitates extra training with the school's technology support staff. Once the curricular unit is complete, the group meets again during the next professional development opportunity to unpack what went well and what did not. Using the SAMR framework, they identify how each teacher envisioned using the simulations, how the simulations were actually implemented, and ways to better use them in the future. In doing so, it is decided that students will work collaboratively next time, and compare their results with other teams. Mariana also completes the TPACK assessment again, to gauge if and how going through this collaborative design and implementation process has helped members of her group become more knowledgeable about the use of technologies to support subject-matter learning.

This same process can be repeated in the future for other identified topics, as well. Over time, some aspects, such as the use of the i^5 inventory, can be relaxed as Mariana and her peers develop an understanding of the infrastructure and support available at their school. Periodically, however, as technology paradigms shift and the school's technology infrastructure changes, these steps might need to be revisited. As this process becomes imbedded in the culture of the department and school, opportunities to learn and integrate ideas from inter-departmental peers can also grow.

CLOSING THOUGHTS: FUTURE TRENDS IN EDUCATIONAL TECHNOLOGIES

Any discussion about the use of technology in a specific educational domain has to start with identifying key parts of that domain that are both important and perhaps difficult to teach using traditional instructional methods. Throughout this volume, we have endeavored to build the argument that success in science education depends on helping students

106 Implementing Technologies

develop robust inquiry skills, and triggering and supporting their motivation to do science, all the while assessing them in ways that get at the skills, knowledge, and motivations they are developing over time. This is no easy task, but we have highlighted how various technologies might be used to help support these critical components. We ended the book by highlighting some useful frameworks to help guide the selection and implementation of certain technologies at different levels of scale.

That all being said, we admit that we have only scratched the surface regarding these topics. Entire series of books such as this one have been written digging more deeply into inquiry learning, motivation, technology-based assessment, and technology implementation. We hope that we have provided a jumping-off point to help guide your own future inquiries into these matters.

In closing, we also thought it appropriate to identify a few technology trends on the horizon, as of the printing of this volume, and speculate on ways they may be used to support real science learning, assess what students know and can do, and motivate traditionally disengaged students. Future generations will doubtlessly look back on this section with the benefit of hindsight, so we do ask that readers in the distant future to be kind in their critique of our naiveté and optimism.

Computational Thinking

The ability to use mathematics and computational thinking ("approach to solving problems in a way that can be implemented with a computer"[21]) is a central practice in the Next Generation Science Standards.[3] This makes sense, as mathematical and logical thinking are essential to understanding and

Implementing Technologies 107

making inferences from the data gathered in inquiry-based curricular activities central to what we have defined as *learning real science*. As such, researchers and instructional designers have begun to produce and test technology-enhanced learning environments meant specifically to enhance these skills.

One example is the Computational Thinking in Simulation and Modeling (CTSiM) learning environment, intended for use in K–12 science classrooms. In a series of studies, Satadbi Basu and her colleagues at Vanderbilt University have demonstrated that middle school science students can simultaneously learn computational thinking skills (such as model building and testing) and science content knowledge while using CTSiM.[22, 23] They also identified potential challenges students might face in learning computational thinking and content knowledge synergistically, and hypothesized potential supports.[23] While this research on integrating computational thinking into science may be in the early stages, it is definitely a growing one. There seems to be strong evidence that using technologies might help support computational thinking as a component of *learning real science*, which given the level to which computers are embedded in scientific careers and research, makes sense.

Furthermore, emphasis in this area is about equalizing opportunities for students from a broad range of backgrounds, an emphasis that we hope we have made clear we are passionate, since computer science suffers from a more dramatic equity pipeline issue than does science.[24] It seems fruitless to work on equalizing who becomes scientists while ignoring the same problem about who becomes computer scientists, given how connected these fields are. We have stated previously that gender, racial, and SES differences in science begin by middle school. Thus, while we are excited about this new

108 Implementing Technologies

line of research and design for students, we are equally glad that it is also extending into preservice and in-service elementary teacher education.[25, 26]

Stealth Assessment

In earlier sections, we highlighted the SAVE Science IVE that one of us (Ketelhut) developed and tested as an assessment platform for science inquiry skills. Some of the data used to assess students were the result of students answering questions within the virtual environment. These are *direct* measures of various aspects of student understanding. However, students also generated data based on their behaviors as they interacted with agents and objects in the virtual environment. These measures can then be used to conduct *stealth* assessments of student understanding of simple and complex traits, such as inquiry.[27]

The concept of stealth assessment, largely pioneered by Val Shute and her colleagues at Florida State University, holds that student competencies can be diagnosed by carefully tracking and measuring student behaviors that correlate with skill development and knowledge over time. Because they do not know that they are being directly assessed, students are more likely to remain engaged and motivated as they complete tasks in various learning environments.[28, 29] As Shute and her colleagues continue to refine and validate these assessments in various science-based games,[30] the potential of this assessment paradigm continues to grow.

Augmented Realities

The individual and multi-user virtual environments we have highlighted throughout this volume are similar to traditional video games, which initially students could only interact

Implementing Technologies   109

with at computers or work stations. More recently, these environments have been moving to tablets as these become more ubiquitous in K–12 education. However, most of these environments are still completely simulated, that is they are separated from the real world. However, with the ubiquity of smartphones, developers have begun harnessing the ability of phones and tablets to be mobile to allow players to simultaneously interact with the virtual and real world while exploring and completing game-based tasks. This represents *augmented reality*. In augmented reality, students view the real world through their phone's viewfinder, and the software then adds virtual information, characters, and items to what might be seen with the naked eye.

A vivid example of the motivational power of augmented reality, when done well, was the wildly popular mobile game "Pokémon Go." We encourage you to search YouTube for "Pokémon Go rare spawn," for example. In the summer of 2016, it was not uncommon to see hundreds of people walking through real world spaces such as parks, while looking through their phones. These 'strollers' were trying to capture digital creatures in the park that they could only see through their phone. The phones were allowing the real world to be augmented by virtual creatures and arenas. Computer games are no longer limited to an indoor space!

The benefits of augmented reality in science education settings have been the focus of Eric Klopfer and his colleagues at MIT. As mobile devices have become ever more powerful, researchers such as Klopfer have worked to build and evaluate engaging learning environments that would allow teachers to embed guided problem-based curricula into real-world settings, offering affordances to learning not possible in more traditional curricula.[31] As technologies continue to evolve,

110 Implementing Technologies

as researchers and designers continue to test and implement best practices, there is a very good chance that augmented realities will play a more central role in fostering motivation in authentic science learning curricula.

REFERENCES

1. Inan, F. A., & Lowther, D. L. (2010). Factors affecting technology integration in K–12 classrooms: A path model. *Educational Technology Research and Development*, 58(2), 137–154.
2. ISTE. (2017). *ISTE standards*. Retrieved March 2, 2017, from www.iste.org/standards/standards/iste-standards
3. NGSS Lead States. (2013). *Next generation science standards: For states, by states.* Washington, DC: National Academies Press.
4. Deck, A. (2015). *How to manage mobile use in the classroom*. Retrieved March 2, 2017, from http://en.community.dell.com/dell-blogs/direct2dell/b/direct2dell/archive/2015/09/22/how-to-manage-mobile-use-in-the-classroom
5. Blythe, T., & Perkins, D. (1998). Understanding understanding. In T. Blythe (Ed.), *The teaching for understanding guide* (pp. 9–16). San Francisco: Jossey-Bass.
6. Wiske, M. S., Rennebohm Franz, K., & Breit, L. (2004). *Teaching for understanding with technology*. San Francisco: Jossey-Bass.
7. Wiggins, G. P., McTighe, J., Kiernan, L. J., Frost, F., & Association for Supervision and Curriculum Development. (1998). *Understanding by design*. Alexandria, VA: Association for Supervision and Curriculum Development.
8. Ball, D. L., & Cohen, D. K. (1996). Reform by the book: What is—or might be—the role of curriculum materials in teacher learning and instructional reform? *Educational Researcher*, 25(6–8), 14.
9. Metcalf, S. J., Tutwiler, M. S., Kamarainen, A., Grotzer, T. A., & Dede, C. J. (2013, April 28). *Multi-user virtual environments to promote middle school ecosystem science learning and attitudes about science*. San Francisco: American Educational Research Association (AERA).
10. Tutwiler, M. S. (2014). *Trends in the salience of data collected in a multi-user virtual environment: An exploratory study*. Unpublished dissertation at the Harvard Graduate School of Education.

Implementing Technologies 111

11. Koehler, M. J., & Mishra, P. (2009). What is technological pedagogical content knowledge. *Contemporary Issues in Technology and Teacher Education*, 9(1), 60–70.

12. Chai, C. S., Koh, J. H. L., & Tsai, C. C. (2013). A review of technological pedagogical content knowledge. *Educational Technology & Society*, 16(2), 31–51.

13. Voogt, J., Fisser, P., Pareja Roblin, N., Tondeur, J., & van Braak, J. (2013). Technological pedagogical content knowledge—a review of the literature. *Journal of Computer Assisted Learning*, 29(2), 109–121.

14. Desimone, L. M., & Garet, M. S. (2015). Best Practices in Teachers' Professional Development in the United States. *Psychology, Society and Education*, 7(3), 252–263.

15. Schifter, C. C. (2008). *Infusing technology into the classroom: Continuous practice improvement*. Hershey, PA: IGI Global.

16. Moersch, C. (1995). Levels of technology implementation (LoTi): A framework for measuring classroom technology use. *Learning and Leading with Technology*, 23, 40–40.

17. Hall, G. E., Loucks, S. F., Rutherford, W. L., & Newlove, B. W. (1975). Levels of use of the innovation: A framework for analyzing innovation adoption. *Journal of Teacher Education*, 26(1), 52–56.

18. Groff, J., & Mouza, C. (2008). A framework for addressing challenges to classroom technology use. *AACE Journal*, 16(1), 21–46.

19. Puentedura, R. R. (2014). *SAMR and TPCK: A hands-on approach to classroom practice*. Presentation slides presented at the 1C Learning Conference, Hong Kong.

20. Shapley, K., Maloney, C., Caranikas-Walker, F., & Sheehan, D. (2008). *Evaluation of the Texas Technology Immersion Pilot: Third-year (2006–07) traits of higher Technology Immersion schools and teachers*. Austin, TX: Texas Center for Educational Research.

21. Stephenson, C., & Barr, V. (2012). Defining computational thinking for K–12. In P. Phillips (Ed.), *Computer science in K-8: Building a strong foundation* (pp. 4–5). New York: Computer Science Teachers Association. Retrieved March 30, 2015, from http://csta.acm.org/Curriculum/sub/CurrFiles/CS_K-8_Building_a_Foundation.pdf

22. Basu, S., Biswas, G., Sengupta, P., Dickes, A., Kinnebrew, J. S., & Clark, D. (2016). Identifying middle school students' challenges in computational thinking-based science learning. *Research and Practice in Technology Enhanced Learning*, 11(1), 13.

112 **Implementing Technologies**

23. Basu, S., Biswas, G., & Kinnebrew, J. S. (2016). Using multiple representations to simultaneously learn computational thinking and middle school science. In *Proceedings of the Thirtieth AAAI Conference on Artificial Intelligence* (pp. 3705–3711). Palo Alto, CA: AAAI Press.

24. Exploring Computer Science. (2016). Retrieved from www.exploringcs.org/resources/cs-statistics

25. Dagher, Z. R., Mouza, C., & Pollock, L. (2017, April 25) *Promoting computational thinking in elementary pre-service science teacher education*. Paper presented at the NARST international conference, San Antonio, Texas.

26. Ketelhut, D. J., McGinnis, J. R., & Plane, J. (2017). *Exploring the integration of computational thinking into preservice elementary science teacher education*. NSF Award Abstract. Retrieved June 30, 2017, from www.nsf.gov/awardsearch/showAward?AWD_ID=1639891&HistoricalAwards=false

27. Gong, X., Mill, K., Bergey, B., Ketelhut, D. J., & Coon, A. (2016, April 8). *How prior knowledge and self-efficacy influence multiple indicators of student performance in virtual environments*. Paper presented at the annual meeting of the AERA conference, Washington, DC.

28. Shute, V. J. (2011). Stealth assessment in computer-based games to support learning. *Computer Games and Instruction, 55*(2), 503–524.

29. Shute, V. J., & Ventura, M. (2013). *Measuring and supporting learning in games: Stealth assessment*. Cambridge, MA: MIT Press.

30. Shute, V. J., & Moore, G. R. (2017). Consistency and validity in game-based stealth assessment. In *Technology enhanced innovative assessment: Development, modeling, and scoring from an interdisciplinary perspective*. Charlotte, NC: Information Age.

31. Duh, H. B., & Klopfer, E. (2013). Augmented reality learning. *Computers & Education, 68*(C), 534–535.

Glossary

Augmented Reality The use of virtual environments on mobile devices to highlight or add features to the real world.

Backwards Design The process of designing curriculum by starting with the desired outcomes.

Bloom's Taxonomy A method for classifying learning objectives from simple to most complex. Originally, six levels were identified: Knowledge, Comprehension, Application, Analysis, Synthesis, and Evaluation (in order of increasing complexity). These were revised in 2001 to be Remember, Understand, Apply, Analyze, Evaluate, and Create.

Computational Thinking A way of thinking that frames problems in a way that computers can help solve.

Discrepant Event A startling outcome that flies in the face of a person's preconceived ideas.

Fixed Mindset The belief that intelligence and abilities are set and unalterable. The opposite of growth mindset.

Formative Assessment Assessment conducted during learning to evaluate how well students are learning and how efficacious teaching practices are. The ultimate goal

114 Glossary

Growth Mindset

Immersive Technology

Immersive Virtual Environment (IVE)

Incremental Theory of Ability

Individualizing Inventory for Integrating Instructional Innovations (i5)

International Society for Technology in Education (ISTE)

Multi-user Virtual Environment (MUVE)

National Science Education Standards (NSES)

of formative assessment is to identify modifications needed in curriculum or pedagogy to improve student learning.

The belief that one can learn over time, and that abilities can change if the required work is done.

Technology that makes the user feel as if they are absorbed in the experience.

A digital environment, often three-dimensional, that a user can explore via an avatar. Often a computer-interface similar to a video game, a user has a sense of being in the environment. Synonym for Growth Mindset.

A framework for identifying potential areas the might block integration of a technological innovation into the classroom.

An international non-profit organization that promotes successful integration of technology for learning.

A virtual world that a user explores simultaneously with other users. Users can usually communicate, 'chat,' with other users during the experience.

K–12 science standards established by the National Research Council of the United States in 1996. They were replaced by the Next Generation Science Standards.

Glossary 115

Next Generation Science Standards (NGSS)	Based on the National Research Council of the United States report in 2011, Framework for K–12 Science Education, these science standards were designed by a coalition of states, including education leaders and teachers, in 2013. They replaced NSES.
Performance assessment	A category of assessment where students complete a task to show understanding as opposed to responding to a multiple choice question.
Portfolios	A form of performance assessment, portfolios usually include a compendium of completed work that purport to indicate a student's level of understanding.
Scientific Inquiry	The many ways that scientists study the natural world and use evidence to propose explanations.
Self-efficacy	The belief that one can succeed in specific situations or accomplish specific tasks.
Situated Theory of Learning	A theory of learning stemming from two teams (Lave and Wenger; Collins, Brown and Duguid) that posits that learning is embedded in a specific context, and thus the most efficacious learning happens in a context most similar to where the knowledge will be used.
Stealth Assessment	Determining what skills students possess or what knowledge they have by examining their behaviors as they complete complex tasks.

116 Glossary

Substitution, Augmentation, Modification, and Redefinition (SAMR)	A framework for monitoring the progress of implementation of a specific technology.
Teaching for Understanding (TfU)	A framework for designing lessons with understanding as the goal; it helps identify key points where technology integration can aid learning.
Technological Pedagogical Content Knowledge (TPACK)	The identification of the key knowledge domains that a teacher needs to have in order to integrate technology seamlessly to enhance the teaching of content knowledge from a specific domain.
Technology Immersion Model (TIM)	A framework for identifying the supports needed to scaffold a top-down (administrator to teacher) technology implementation.
Validity	The determination of how well a test measures what it says it measures.

Acknowledgments

The authors wish to acknowledge that some of the material in this book is based upon work supported by the National Science Foundation. We would also like to thank the various team members that worked with us on the various research projects mentioned throughout this book. Our ideas were forged in discussions, debates, and collaborations with you!

Index

Boldface page references indicate tables. *Italic* references indicate figures.

ability in science 74–77
adaptation example in test design 49–52
Alberts, B. 9–12, 17–18, 64–65, 71
American Association for the Advancement of Science 15
assessment: context and, lack of 48–52, 60; formative 38, 46; learning and 33; motivation and 65; performance 46–47, 54–55, 60; stealth 108
assessment issue: assessment outcomes and 35–36, *36*, 52; biases 53; comprehensive assessment of science learning goals and 37–42; conceptual understanding and 18, 42–47; context, lack of 48–52, 60; false negatives 48; false positives 47–48; historical perspective 33–34; ICESE framework and 53–57; impact of test design and 42–53; learning goals and 35–37, *36*; material tested and 53; measurement and 34–35; National Science Education
Standards and 39; overview 5–6, 60; quantification and 34–35; SAVE science (Situated Assessment using Virtual Environment for Science) and 57–60; science assessment framework 53–57; standardized tests and 33–34, 38–39; teaching focus and 33, 35–37, *36*; teaching to the test and 36–37, 44–45; technology in improving 55–60; test design and 35–37, *36*; unassessed knowledge and 45–46; *see also* test design
augmented realities 108–110
authenticity 8–9, 56–57
authentic scientific work 8

Backwards Design 91
Bandura, A. 66, 68
biases 53
Bloom's Taxonomy 42–43, *43*, 46

'canned' curricula 88
Carnegie Foundation report (2009) 41, 46, 48, 54

Index 119

collaborative online platforms 100
comprehensive assessment of
science learning goals 37–42
computational thinking 106–108
Computational Thinking in
Simulation and Modeling
(CTSiM) 107
conceptual understanding 18,
25–26, 42–47
contextualization: equity issues
and 50–53; immersive
technology and 56–57; lack
of, in assessment 48–52, 60;
portfolios and 54–55
critical thinking 4–5
critiques of educational system
1–2
curriculum: 'canned' 88;
implementing technology into
classrooms and 85–91; learning
goals and design of 37–42;
outdated 88–89

Dede, C. 89–90
Department of Education 15
Desimone, L. M. 95
Dewey, J. 39
discrepant event 19
Drayton, B. 44
Duvall, R. 21, 28

education: future technology
trends in 105–110; goal of 13;
see also science education
emotional feedback 68–69
empowered professional 89
engagement 9, 45–46, 70–71
equity issues 23–24, 50–53
evaluating information 2–3

experience equals expertise
concept 2
experiences and self-efficacy
68–71
exploring world 8–9, 11–15,
18–20

Facilitators teacher category 92
Falk, J. 44
false negatives 48
false positives 47–48
Fan, X. 73
Federation of American Scientists 4
feedback, emotional 68–69
fixed mindset 75
formative assessment 38, 46

Garet, M. S. 95
Gates, Bill 2
gender differences and interest in
science 72–73
goals: comprehensive assessment
of science learning 37–42;
of education 13; incremental
75–76; learning 35–42, 36
Google Docs 100
Groff, J. 98–99
growth mindset 74–77

hands-on versus 'minds-on' 29
higher order thinking skills 4–5

ICESE framework 53–57
immersive technology: conceptual
understanding and 25–26;
context and, real 56–57;
defining 4, 24
immersive virtual environments
(IVEs) 57–58, 90

120 **Index**

implementing technology into classrooms: augmented realities and 108–110; background information 84–85; Backwards Design and 91; computational thinking and 106–108; curriculum and 85–91; evaluating, frameworks for 97–103; future trends in 105–110; Individualized Inventory for Integrating Instructional Innovation and 98–99; International Society for Technology in Education and 86–89, 91, 104; knowledge types for 93; overview 103–105; pedagogy and 91–97; policy and 85–97; positive effect of, maximizing 93; practice and 85–97; questions involving 85; stealth assessment and 108; structuring guidelines 96–97; Substitution, Augmentation, Modification, and Redefinition and 100–101, **101**, 104; supporting, frameworks for 97–103; teacher categories in 92; Teaching for Understanding framework and 90–91; Technological Pedagogical Content Knowledge and 93–97, 94, 104; Technology Immersion Model 101–103; top-down components 102

incremental goals 75–76

incremental theory of ability 74–77

Individualized Inventory for Integrating Instructional

Innovation (i^5) framework 98–99

inequity issues 23–24, 50–53

information 2–3

Integrating Instructional Innovations (i^3) framework 99

interest in science 72–74, 79

International Society for Technology in Education (ISTE) 86–89, 91, 104

Jensen, R. A. 73

Jeopardy champions 2–3

Klopfer, E. 109

knowledge: connecting real-world exploration with scientific 11–12; constructor 88; information as 2; for science proficiency 16, 40–41; types for implementing technology into classrooms 93; unassessed 45–46

Koehler, M. J. 93

learning: assessment and 33; contexts and, authentic 49; engagement and 45–46, 70–71; goals 35–42, 36; incremental goals and 76; motivation and 65; opportunities, creating best 67–68; rote 12; technology stagnation of use for 4–5

learning real science issue: computational thinking and 107; defining real science and 8–9; misunderstanding science and 7–8; overview 5–6, 29–30; school science versus real science and 9–12;

Index 121

scientific inquiry and 12–16, 107; technology in improving 24–29, **28**, 107
Liu, C. 73

McMullen, D. 73
Maltese, A. 73
mastery experiences and self-efficacy 68–71
Mazur, E. 11
measurement 34–35
mentor teachers 22–23
Metcalf, S. 92
Michael, J. 48
'minds-on' 29
Mishra, P. 93
mobile devices 109
Moersch, C. 98
Monitors teacher category 92
motivation issues: assessment and 65; augmented reality and 110; current approach to school science and 64–65; growth mindset and 74–77; interest in science and 72–74; learning and 65; overview 5–6, 79–80; self-efficacy and 66–71, 77; technology in improving 77–79
Mouza, C. 98–99
multiple choice test design 42, 44, 46–47, 51, 54, 56, 59–60
multi-user virtual environment (MUVE) 92

National Assessment of Educational Progress (NAEP) 69, 72
National Research Council (NRC) 15–16, 39–41
National Science Board 7

National Science Education Standards (NSES) 21, 39
Next Generation Science Standards (NGSS) 16, 20, 21, 40–42, 88, 101, 104

outdated curricula 88–89

Pajares, F. 67
pedagogy and implementing technology into classrooms 91–97
performance assessment 46–47, 54–55, 60
personal experiences and self-efficacy 68–71
persuasion, verbal 68
Piaget, J. 12, 15, 18
pipeline in science 72–73
playing *see* exploring world
Pokémon Go mobile game 109
policy and implementing technology into classrooms 85–97
portfolios 46, 54–55
positive experiences 68, 71
practice and implementing technology into classrooms 85–97
problem solving 2–3
proficiency in science, knowledge for 16, 40–41
pseudo-scientific inquiry 21–22
Puentedura, R. 100

quantification 34–35
Quest Atlantis internet-based game 29

real science: authenticity and 8–9; defining 8–9; school science versus 7–12; *see also* learning real science issue

122 Index

recipes, following 14–15
reliability 46–47, 54–55, 58
River City internet-based game 26–29, **28**, 78–79

Sages teacher category 92
SAVE science (Situated Assessment using Virtual Environment for Science) 57–60, 108
school science: Alberts and 9–12, 64–65; current approach to 9–12, 64–65; engagement in, varying 9; exploring world versus 11–15; inquiry-based 21; knowledge for science proficiency and 40–41; national standards for 16, 20–21, 40–42, 88, 101, 106; purpose of 10–11; real science versus 7–12; as rote learning exercise 12; scientific inquiry and 12–16, 33, 40; telling students and 14; *see also* science education
science education: categories of issues in 5–6; mentor teachers and 22–23; overview 3–6; teachers' major in 22; vision of 3; *see also* school science; *specific learning issue*
science and engineering practices 88, 101
science learning issues *see* assessment issue; learning real science issue; motivation issue
scientific inquiry: defining 12–13; 'divide' 23–24; engagement and 45–46, 70–71; exploring world and 12–15, 18–20; failure to integrate into classroom 16–24,
43–44; importance of 12, 39; inequity of implementing in classroom 16, 23–24; lack of understanding of importance of 16–20; 'light' 22; mastery experiences and 71; misunderstanding in classroom 16, 20–23; national standards for engaging in 21, 23; policy doctrines for 16; pseudo 21–22; *Quest Atlantis* internet-based game and 29; *River City* internet-based game and 26–29, 28; school science and 12–16, 33, 40, 107; self-efficacy and 70–71; test design and assessing 42; test design and implementing in classroom 43–44; textbooks and 22
scientific literacy of populace 7, 67
Scientopolis internet-based game 57–58, 59
self-efficacy 66–71, 77
Shute, V. 108
SimCity video game 3–4
situated context 51
situated theory 49
Spencer, H. 15
standardized tests 33–34, 38–39
state tests 33–34
stealth assessment 108
STEM careers 72–73
Substitution, Augmentation, Modification, and Redefinition (SAMR) framework 100–101, **101**, 104
successful experiences 68
success and growth mindset 75–77

Index 123

Tai, R. 73
Taking Science to School (NRC report)
16, 39–41
teaching focus 33, 35–37, 36
teaching to the test 36–37, 44–45
Teaching for Understanding (TfU)
framework 90–91
Technological Pedagogical Content
Knowledge (TPACK) 93–97,
94, 104
technology: assessment issues and,
improving 55–60; classrooms
and 84–85; evolving use of in
education 4; examples, caution
about 5–6; future trends in
educational 105–110; higher
order thinking skills and 4–5;
learning real science issue and,
improving 24–29, **28**, 107;
motivation issue and, improving
77–79; overview 3–4;
stagnation of use for learning in
school 4–5; *see also* immersive
technology; implementing
technology into classrooms
Technology Immersion Model
(TIM) 101–103
technology-in-education books 5
telling students 14
test design: adaptation example
and 49–52; assessment
issue and 35–37, 36;
broad spectrum of 46–47;
components of good 54;

conceptual understanding
assessment and 42–47;
context and, lack of 48–52;
false negatives and 48; false
positives and 47–48; impact
of 42–53; learning goals and
35, 36, 37; multiple choice 42,
44, 46–48, 51, 54, 56, 59–60;
outcome and 35–36, 36, 52;
scientific inquiry assessment
and 42–43; scientific inquiry
implementation in classroom
and 43–44; situated theory
and 49; teaching focus and 36,
36; teaching to the test and
44–45; unassessed knowledge
and 45–46; validity and 50–51
testing 33–34; *see also*
assessment issue
TIMS (Trends in International
Mathematics and Science Study)
assessment 53

ubiquity of information 2
unassessed knowledge 45–46

validity 46–47, 50–51,
54–55, 58
verbal persuasion 68
vicarious experiences 68
Voogt, J. 95

'why' questions 73
Whyville internet-based game 29